The Self-Taught Programmer

Cory Althoff

ISBN 978-0-9996859-0-7
1st Edition
Published by Triangle Connection LLC
http://theselftaughtprogrammer.io

Illustrations by Blake Bowers.
Edited by James Althoff, Steve Bush, Lawrence Sanfilippo, Madeline Luce and Pam Walatka.

I dedicate this book to my parents, Abby and James Althoff, for always supporting me.

Table of Contents

Part I Introduction to Programming

Chapter 3. Introduction to Programming 13

Chapter 4. Functions 47

Chapter 5. Containers 67

Chapter 6. String Manipulation 87

Part II Introduction to Object-Oriented Programming

Chapter 14. More Object-Oriented Programming 163

Chapter 15. Bringing It All Together 171

Part III Introduction to Programming Tools

Part IV Introduction to Computer Science

Part V Landing a Job

Part I
Introduction to Programming

Chapter 1. Introduction

"Most good programmers do programming not because they expect to get paid or get adulation by the public, but because it is fun to program."
—Linus Torvalds

I majored in political science at Clemson University. I considered computer science, and even enrolled in an Introduction to Programming class my freshman year, but quickly dropped it. It was too difficult. While living in Silicon Valley after graduation, I decided I needed to learn to program. A year later, I was working as a software engineer II at eBay (above an entry-level software engineer, but below a senior software engineer). I don't want to give the impression that this was easy. It was incredibly challenging. In between throwing things at the wall, I had a lot of fun.

I started my journey learning to program in Python, a popular programming language. This book, however, is not just about teaching you how to program in a particular language—although it does. It's about everything else the standard resources do not teach you. It's about the things I had to learn on my own to become a software engineer. This book is not for someone looking for a casual introduction to programming so they can write code as a hobby. This book is written specifically for those looking to program professionally. Whether your goal is to become a software engineer, an entrepreneur, or to use your new programming skills in another profession, I wrote this book for you.

Learning a programming language is only part of the battle. There are other skills you need in order to speak the language of computer scientists. I will teach you everything I learned on my journey from programming novice to professional software engineer. I wrote this book to give aspiring programmers an outline of what they need to know. As a self-taught programmer, I didn't know what I needed to learn. The introductions to programming books are all the same. They teach you the basics of how to program in either Python or Ruby, and send you on your way. The feedback I've heard from people finishing these books is "What do I do now? I am not a programmer yet, and I don't know what to learn next." This book is my answer to that question.

How This Book Is Structured

Many of the subjects covered in a single chapter of this book could be—and are—covered by entire books. My goal is not to cover every detail of every subject you need to know. My goal is to give you a map—an outline of all of the skills you need to develop to program professionally. This book is divided into five parts:

Part I: Introduction to Programming. You will write your first program as quickly as possible, hopefully today.

Part II: Introduction to Object-Oriented Programming. I cover the different programming paradigms—focusing on object-oriented programming. You will build a game that shows you the power of programming. You will be hooked on programming after this section.

Part III: Introduction to Programming Tools. You learn to use different tools to take your programming productivity to the next level. At this point, you are hooked on programming and want to get even better. You will learn more about your operating system, how to use regular expressions to boost your productivity, how to install and manage other people's programs, and how to collaborate with other engineers using version control.

Part IV: Introduction to Computer Science. This section is a light introduction to computer science. I cover two important topics: algorithms and data structures.

Part V: Landing a Job. The final section is about best programming practices, getting a job as a software engineer, working on a team, and improving as a programmer. I provide tips on how to pass a technical interview and work on a team, as well as advice on how to further enhance your skills.

If you don't have any programming experience, you should practice programming on your own as much as possible between each section. Don't try to read this book too quickly. Use it as a guide and practice for as long as you need in between sections.

Endgame First

The way I learned to program is the opposite of how computer science is usually taught, and I structured the book to follow my approach. Traditionally, you spend a lot of time learning theory—so much so, that many computer science graduates come out of school not knowing how to program. In his blog "Why Can't Programmers.. Program?," Jeff Atwood writes, "Like me, the author is having trouble with the fact that 199 out of 200 applicants for every programming job can't write code at all. I repeat: they can't write any code whatsoever." This revelation led Atwood to create the **FizzBuzz** coding challenge, a programming test used in interviews to weed out candidates. Most people fail the challenge, and that's why you spend so much of this book learning the skills you will use in practice. Don't worry, you also learn how to pass the FizzBuzz test.

In *The Art of Learning,* Josh Waitzkin of *Searching for Bobby Fischer* fame describes how he learned how to play chess in reverse. Instead of studying opening moves, he started learning the endgame (when there are only a few pieces left on the board) first. This strategy gave him a better understanding of the game, and he went on to win many championships. Similarly, I think it is more efficient to learn to program first, then learn theory later, once you are dying to know how everything works. That is why I wait until Part IV of the book to introduce computer science theory, and I keep it to a minimum. While theory is important, it will be even more valuable once you already have programming experience.

You Are Not Alone

Learning how to program outside of school is increasingly common. A 2015 Stack Overflow (an online community of programmers) survey found 48 percent of respondents did not have a degree in computer science.[1]

The Self-Taught Advantage

When eBay hired me, I was on a team that included programmers with computer science degrees from Stanford, Cal, and Duke, as well as two physics Ph.D's. At 25, it was intimidating that my 21-year-old teammates knew 10 times more about programming and computer science than I did.

As intimidating as it is to work with people who have bachelor's, master's and Ph.Ds in computer science, never forget you have what I like to call the "self-taught advantage." You are not reading this book because a teacher assigned it to you, you are reading it because you have a desire to learn, and wanting to learn is the biggest advantage you can have. Also, don't forget that some of the most successful people in the world are self-taught programmers. Steve Wozniak, the founder of Apple, is a self-taught programmer. So is Margaret Hamilton, who received the Presidential Medal of Freedom for her work on NASA's Apollo Moon missions; David Karp, founder of Tumblr; Jack Dorsey, founder of Twitter; and Kevin Systrom, founder of Instagram.

Why You Should Program

Programming can help your career regardless of your profession. Learning to program is empowering. I love coming up with new ideas, and I always have a new project I want to start. Once I learned to program, I could sit down and build my ideas without needing to find someone to do it for me.

Programming will also make you better at everything else you do. There aren't many subjects that don't benefit from finely tuned problem-solving skills. Recently, I had the very tedious task of searching for housing on Craigslist. I was able to write a program to do the work for me and email me the results. Learning to program will free you from repetitive tasks forever.

If you want to become a software engineer, there is an increasing demand and not enough qualified people to fill the available positions. By 2020, an estimated 1 million programming jobs will go unfilled.[2] Even if your goal isn't to become a software engineer, jobs in fields like science and finance are beginning to favor candidates with programming experience.

Sticking with It

If you don't have any programming experience and are nervous about making this journey, I want you to know you are capable of it. There are some common misconceptions about programmers like they all are great at math. They aren't. You don't need to be great at math to learn to program, but it does take hard work. With that said, a lot of the material covered in this book is easier to learn than you think.

To improve your programming skills, you should practice programming every day. The only thing that will hold you back is not sticking with it, so let's go over two ways to make sure you do.

When I was getting started, I used a checklist to ensure I practiced every day, and it helped me stay focused. You can also sign up for my online programming course, which comes with access to my private Facebook community, at goselftaught.com.

If you need extra help, Tim Ferriss, a productivity expert, recommends the following technique to stay motivated: give money to a friend or family member with instructions to return it to you upon completion of your goal within a given time frame, or donate it to an organization you dislike if you fail.

How This Book Is Formatted

The chapters in this book build on one another. I try to avoid re-explaining concepts, so keep this in mind. Important terms appear in bold when I first introduce them. There is a vocabulary section at the end of each chapter where each bold word is defined. There are also challenges at the end of each chapter to help you develop your programming skills, as well as links to the solutions.

Technologies Used in This Book

This book teaches certain technologies to give you as much practical programming experience as possible. I try to be technology agnostic, focusing on concepts instead of technologies.

In some cases, I had to choose between many different technologies. In Chapter 20: "Version Control" (for those readers who are unfamiliar with version control, I will explain later), I go over the basics of using Git, a popular version control system. I chose Git because I consider it the industry standard for version control. I use Python for the majority of the programming examples, because it is a popular programming language to learn, and it is a very easy language to read, even if you have never used it. There is also a huge demand for Python developers in just about every field.

To follow the examples in this book, you will need a computer. Your computer has an **operating system**—a program that is the middleman between the physical components of the computer and you. What you see when you look at your computer screen is called a **graphical user interface** or GUI, which is part of your operating system.

There are three popular operating systems for desktop and laptop computers: **Windows**, **Unix**, and **Linux**. Windows is Microsoft's operating system. Unix is an operating system created in the 1970s. Apple's current operating system is based on Unix. From here on out, when I refer to Unix, I am referring to Apple's desktop operating system. Linux is an **open-source** operating system used by the majority of the world's **servers**. A server is a computer or computer program that performs tasks, like hosting a website. Open-source means a company or individual does not own the software and it may be redistributed and modified. Linux and Unix are both **Unix-like operating systems**, which means they are very similar. This book assumes you are using a computer running Windows, Unix, or Ubuntu (a popular version of Linux) as your operating system.

Vocabulary

FizzBuzz: A programming test used in interviews to weed out candidates.
Operating system: A program that is the middleman between the physical components of the computer and you.
Graphical user interface (GUI): The part of your operating system you see when you look at your computer screen.
Windows: Microsoft's operating system.

Unix: An operating system created in the 1970s. Apple's operating system is based on Unix.

Linux: An open-source operating system used by the majority of the world's servers.

Open-source: Software that is not owned by a company or individual, but is instead maintained by a group of volunteers.

Server: A computer or computer program that performs tasks, like hosting a website.

Unix-like operating systems: Unix and Linux.

Challenge

1. Create a daily checklist that includes practicing programming.

Chapter 2. Getting Started

"A good programmer is someone who always looks both ways before crossing a one-way street."
—Doug Linder

What Is Programming

Programming is writing instructions for a computer to execute. The instructions might tell the computer to print `Hello, World!`, scrape data from the Internet, or read the contents of a file and save them to a database. These instructions are called **code**. Programmers write code in many different programming languages. In the past, programming was much harder, as programmers were forced to use cryptic, **low-level programming languages** like **assembly language**. When a programming language is low-level, it is closer to being written in binary (0s and 1s) than a **high-level programming language** (a programming language that reads more like English), and thus is harder to understand. Here is a simple program written in an assembly language:

```
# http://tinyurl.com/z6facmk


global    _start
          section .text
_start:
          mov       rax, 1
          mov       rdi, 1
          mov       rsi, message
          mov       rdx, 13
          syscall
          ; exit(0)
          mov       eax, 60
          xor       rdi, rdi
          syscall
message:
          db        "Hello, World!", 10
```

Here is the same program written in a modern programming language:

```
1  # http://tinyurl.com/zhj8ap6
2
3
4  print("Hello, World!")
```

As you can see, programmers today have it much easier. You won't need to spend time learning cryptic, low-level programming languages to program. Instead, you will learn an easy-to-read programming language called Python.

What Is Python

Python is an open-source programming language created by Dutch programmer Guido van Rossum, named after the British sketch comedy group Monty Python. One of van Rossum's key insights was that programmers spend more time reading code than writing it, so he created an easy-to-read language. Python is one of the most popular and easiest to learn programming languages in the world. It runs on all the major operating systems and computers and is used to build web servers, create desktop applications, and everything in between. Because of its popularity, there is a significant demand for Python programmers.

Installing Python

To follow the examples in this book, you need to have Python Version 3 installed. You can download Python for Windows and Unix at http://python.org/downloads. If you are on Ubuntu, Python 3 comes installed by default. **Make sure you download Python 3, not Python 2. Some of the examples in this book will not work if you are using Python 2.**

Python is available for 32-bit and 64-bit computers. If you purchased your computer after 2007, it is most likely a 64-bit computer. If you aren't sure, an Internet search should help you figure it out.

If you are on Windows or a Mac, download the 32- or 64-bit version of Python, open the file, and follow the instructions. You can also visit http://theselftaughtprogrammer. io/installpython for videos explaining how to install Python on each operating system.

Troubleshooting

From this point forward, you need to have Python installed. If you are having problems installing Python, please skip ahead to Chapter 11 to the section titled "Getting Help."

The Interactive Shell

Python comes with a program called IDLE, short for interactive development environment (also the last name of Eric Idle, one of the members of Monty Python's Flying Circus). IDLE is where you will be typing your Python code. Once you've downloaded Python, search for IDLE in Explorer (PC), Finder (Mac), or Nautilus (Ubuntu). I recommend creating a desktop shortcut to make it easy to find.

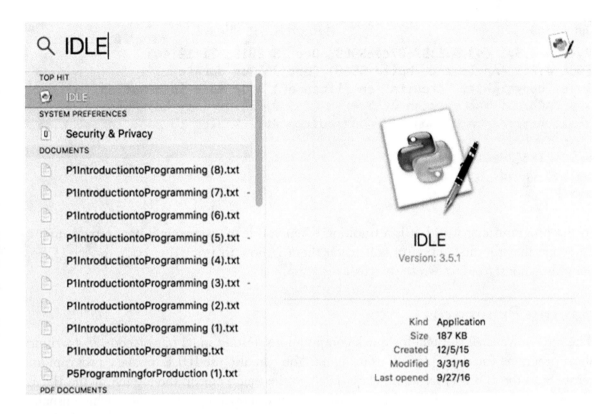

Click on the IDLE icon, and a program with the following lines will open (although this could change, so don't worry if the message is absent or different):

Python 3.5.1 (v3.5.1:37a07cee5969, Dec 5 2015, 21:12:44) [GCC 4.2.1 (Apple Inc. build 5666) (dot 3)] on darwin Type "copyright", "credits" or "license()" for more information. >>>

This program is called the interactive shell. You can type Python code directly into the interactive shell, and it will print the results. At the prompt >>> type:

```
1  print("Hello, World!")
```

Then press enter.

IDLE might reject code copied from Kindle, other eBooks, or word processors like Microsoft Word. If you copy and paste code and get an unexplainable error message, try typing the code directly into the shell. You must type the code exactly as written in the example, including quotation marks, parentheses, and any other punctuation.

The interactive shell will respond by printing Hello, World!

```
● ● ●                    Python 3.5.1 Shell
Python 3.5.1 (v3.5.1:37a07cee5969, Dec  5 2015, 21:12:44)
[GCC 4.2.1 (Apple Inc. build 5666) (dot 3)] on darwin
Type "copyright", "credits" or "license()" for more information.
>>> WARNING: The version of Tcl/Tk (8.5.9) in use may be unstable.
Visit http://www.python.org/download/mac/tcltk/ for current information.

>>> print("Hello, World!")
Hello, World!
>>> |
```

In the programming world, it is a tradition when you teach someone a new programming language that the first program you teach them is how to print Hello, World! So, congratulations! You just wrote your first program.

Saving Programs

The interactive shell is useful for quick computations, testing small bits of code and writing short programs you don't plan on using again. You can also use IDLE to save a program for reuse. Start the IDLE application, click "File" (in the menu bar on the top left of the IDLE editor), then select "New File." Selecting this option will open up a text editor, which usually has a blank white background. You can write code in this text editor and save it to run later. When you run your code, the output will appear in the interactive shell. You need to save changes while editing code before running it again. Type the Hello, World! program into the text editor:

```
● ● ●                                          *Untitled*
```

Go to "File" again and select "Save As." Name your file "hello_world.py" and save it. Python file names have to end with .py. Once you've saved your file, click "Run" (in the menu bar in the top left corner of the IDLE editor), and select "Run Module." Alternatively, you can press the F5 key command, the equivalent of selecting "Run Module" from the menu bar. Hello, World! will print in the interactive shell, as if you had typed this line of code. But now, since you saved your program, you can run it as many times as you like.

The program you created is simply a file with a .py extension, located on your computer wherever you saved it. The name I chose for the file—"hello_world.py"—is completely arbitrary, you can name the file anything. Like this example, writing programs in Python simply involves typing text into files and running them using the interactive shell. Easy, right?

Running Example Programs

Throughout the book, I give examples of code and the results that print when you run them. Whenever I do this, you should enter the code and run it yourself.

Short examples are best run using the shell, and the text editor is better for longer programs you want to save and edit. If you make a mistake in your code in the interactive shell a typo for example—and the code doesn't work, you have to type everything over again. Using the text editor lets you save your work, so if you make a mistake, you simply fix it and rerun the program.

Another reason the distinction is important is the output of a program running from a file versus the shell can be slightly different. If you type `100` into the interactive shell and press enter, the interactive shell will output `100`. If you type `100` into a .py file and run it, there will be no output. This difference can cause confusion, so be mindful of where you are running a program from if you do not get the same output as the example.

Vocabulary

Programming: Writing instructions for a computer to execute.
Code: The instructions programmers write for a computer to execute.
Low-level programming language: A programming language closer to being written in binary (0s and 1s) than a high-level programming language.
Assembly language: A type of difficult-to-read programming language.
High-level programming language: A programming language that reads more like English than a low-level programming language.
Python: The easy-to-read, open-source programming language you will learn to use in this book. Created by Guido van Rossum and named after the British sketch comedy group Monty Python.

Challenge

1. Try to print something other than `Hello, World!`.

Solution: http://tinyurl.com/noeujfu.

Chapter 3. Introduction to Programming

"It's the only job I can think of where I get to be both an engineer and an artist. There's an incredible, rigorous, technical element to it, which I like because you have to do very precise thinking. On the other hand, it has a wildly creative side where the boundaries of imagination are the only real limitation."
—Andy Hertzfeld

Our irst program printed `Hello, World!` Let's print it a hundred times. Type the following code into the interactive shell (print needs to be indented exactly four spaces):

```
1  # http://tinyurl.com/h79ob7s
2
3
4  for i in range(100):
5      print("Hello, World!")
```

Your shell should print `Hello, World!` a hundred times. Even though you will probably never need to print `Hello, World!` a hundred times, this example shows you how powerful programming is. Can you think of anything else you can do a hundred times so easily? I can't. That is the power of programming.

Examples

From now on, code examples will look like this:

```
1  # http://tinyurl.com/h4qntgk
2
3
4  for i in range(100):
5      print("Hello, World!")
```

```
>> Hello, World!
>> Hello, World!
>> Hello, World!
...
```

The text # http://tinyurl.com/h4qntgk contains a URL that takes you to a web page that contains the code from it, so you can easily copy and paste it into the IDLE text editor if you are having problems getting the code to run. The text that comes after >> is the output of the interactive shell. Throughout the book, you will see >> after each programming example, which represents the output of the program (printed in the interactive shell). Ellipses (. . .) mean "and so on."

If there is no >> after an example, it means either the program doesn't produce an output, or I am explaining a concept and the output is not important.

Anything written in `Courier New` font is some form of code, code output or programming jargon. For example, if I refer to the word `for` in the previous example, it will be written in the `Courier New` font.

Courier New is a fix-width (non-proportional) font often used to display programming text. Each character has the same width, so indentation and other display characteristics of code alignment are easier to observe.

You can run examples from either the shell or a `.py` file. Be aware that, as I mentioned earlier, the output from the shell is slightly different so if you are not getting the same output, that is why. If an example prints an output but doesn't have the word `print` in it, you should enter the code into the shell. If the word `print` is in an example, you should run the code from a .py file.

Comments

A **comment** is a line (or part of a line) of code written in English (or another language), preceded by a symbol telling the programming language you are using to ignore that line (or part of a line) of code. In Python, the pound symbol is used to create comments.

A comment explains what a line of code does. Programmers use comments to make the line of code easier to understand for whoever reads it. You can write whatever you want in a comment, as long as it is only one line long:

```
1  # http://tinyurl.com/hut6nwu
2
3  # This is a comment
4  print("Hello, World!")
```

```
>> Hello, World!
```

Only write a comment if you are doing something unusual in your code, or explaining something that is not obvious in the code itself. Use comments sparingly—do not comment on every line of code you write—save them for special situations. Here is an example of an unnecessary comment:

```
1  # http://tinyurl.com/jpzlwqq
2
3
4  # print Hello, World!
5  print("Hello, World!")
```

It is unnecessary because it is already very clear what the line of code does. Here is an example of a good comment:

```
1   # http://tinyurl.com/z52c8z8
2
3
4   import math
5
6
7   # length of a diagonal
8   l = 4
9   w = 10
10  d = math.sqrt(l**2 + w**2)
```

Even if you understood exactly how this code works, you still might not know how to calculate the length of a diagonal of a rectangle, so the comment is useful.

Printing

You are not limited to printing Hello, World! in your programs. You can print whatever you'd like, as long as you surround it with quotes:

```
1  # http://tinyurl.com/zh5g2a3
2
3
4  print("Python")
```

```
>> Python
```

```
1  # http://tinyurl.com/hhwqva2
2
3
4  print("Hola!")
```

```
>> Hola!
```

Lines

Python programs are made up of lines of code. Take a look at this program:

```
1  # http://tinyurl.com/jq2w5ro
2
3
4  # line1
5  # line2
6  # line3
```

There are three lines of code. It is useful to refer to each piece of code by the line it is on. In IDLE, you can go to "Edit" and select "Go to Line" to jump to a particular line in your program. You can only enter one line of code into the shell at once. You cannot copy and paste multiple lines.

Sometimes a piece of code is long and takes up more than one line. Code surrounded by three quotes, parentheses, brackets and braces can extend to a new line:

```
1  # http://tinyurl.com/zcdx3yo
2
3
4  print("""This is a really really
5           really really long line of
6           code.""")
```

You can use a backward slash \ to extend code to the next line when you wouldn't normally be able to:

```
1  # http://tinyurl.com/hjcf2sa
2
3
4  print\
5  ("""This is a really really
6   really long line of code.""")
```

This example and the previous example have the same output. The slash allowed me to put ("""This is a really really really long line of code.""") and print on separate lines, which otherwise is not allowed.

Keywords

Programming languages like Python have words with special meanings, called **keywords**. for, a keyword you've already seen, is used to execute code multiple times. You will learn more keywords throughout this chapter.

Spacing

Let's take another look at your program that prints Hello, World! a hundred times:

```
1  # http://tinyurl.com/glp9xq6
2
3
4  for i in range(100):
5      print("Hello, World!")
```

As I noted earlier, print is indented four spaces. I will cover why shortly, but it lets Python know when blocks of code begin and end. In the meantime, please be aware that whenever you see an indent in an example, it is an indent of four spaces. Without proper spacing, your program will not work.

Other programming languages do not use spacing like this; they use keywords or brackets instead. Here is the same program written in another programming language called JavaScript:

```
 1   # http://tinyurl.com/hwa2zae
 2
 3
 4   # This is a JavaScript program.
 5   # It will not work.
 6
 7
 8   for (i = 0; i < 100; i++) {
 9       console.log("Hello, World!");
10   }
```

Python proponents believe the required use of proper spacing makes Python less tedious to read and write than other languages. Like in the example above, even when space is not part of the programming language, programmers include it to make their code easier to read.

Data Types

Python groups data into different categories called **data types**. In Python, each data value, like 2 or "Hello, World!", is called an **object**. You will learn more about objects in Part II, but for now think of an object as a data value in Python with three properties: identity, data type, and value. An object's identity is its location in your computer's memory, which never changes. The data type of an object is the category of data the object belongs to, which determines the properties the object has and never changes. The value of an object is the data it represents—the number 2, for example, has a value of 2.

"Hello, World!" is an object with the data type **str**, short for **string**, and the value "Hello, World!". When you refer to an object with the data type str, you call it a string. A string is a sequence of one or more characters surrounded by quotes. A **character** is a single symbol like a or 1. You can use single quotes or double quotes, but the quotes at the beginning and end of a string must match:

```
 1   # http://tinyurl.com/hh5kjwp
 2
 3
 4   "Hello, World!"
```

```
>> 'Hello, World!'
```

```
1  # http://tinyurl.com/heaxhsh
2
3
4  'Hello, World!'

>> 'Hello, World!'
```

Strings are used to represent text, and they have unique properties.

The numbers you used to do math in the previous section are also objects—but they are not strings. Whole numbers (1, 2, 3, 4, etc.) have the data type int, short for **integer**. Like strings, integers have unique properties. For example, you can multiply two integers, but you cannot multiply two strings.

Decimal numbers (numbers with a decimal point) have a data type called float. 2.1, 8.2, and 9.9999 are all objects with the float data type. They are called **floating-point numbers**. Like all data types, floating-point numbers have unique properties and behave in a certain way, similarly to integers:

```
1  # http://tinyurl.com/guoc4gy
2
3
4  2.2 + 2.2

>> 4.4
```

Objects with a bool data type are called **booleans**, and have a value of True or False:

```
1  # http://tinyurl.com/jyllj2k
2
3
4  True

>> True
```

```
1  # http://tinyurl.com/jzgsxz4
2
3
4  False

>> False
```

Objects with a data type **NoneType** always have the value **None**. They are used to represent the absence of value:

```
1  # http://tinyurl.com/h8oqo5v
2
3
4  None
```

I explain how to use the different data types throughout this chapter.

Constants and Variables

You can use Python to do math, just like you would a calculator. You can add, subtract, divide, multiply, raise a number to a power, and much more. Remember to type all of the examples in this section into the shell.

```
1  # http://tinyurl.com/zs65dp8
2
3
4  2 + 2
```

>> 4

```
1  # http://tinyurl.com/gs9nwrw
2
3
4  2 - 2
```

>> 0

```
1  # http://tinyurl.com/hasegvj
2
3
4  4 / 2
```

>> 2.0

```
1  # http://tinyurl.com/z8ok4q3
2
3
4  2 * 2
```

>> 4

A **constant** is a value that never changes. Each of the numbers in the previous example is a constant; the number two will always represent the value 2. A **variable**, on the other hand, refers to a value that can change. A variable consists of a name made up of one or more characters. That name is assigned a value using the **assignment operator** (the = sign).

Some programming languages require the programmer to include variable "declarations" that tell the programming language what data type the variable will be. For example, in the C programming language, you create a variable like this:

```
1  # Do not run.
2
3
4
5
6
7  int a;
8  a = 144;
```

Python makes it simpler; you create a variable simply by assigning a value to it with the assignment operator:

```
1  # http://tinyurl.com/hw64mrr
2
3
4  b = 100
5  b
```

```
>> 100
```

Here is how to change the value of a variable:

```
1  # http://tinyurl.com/hw97que
2
3
4  x = 100
5  x
6
7
8  x = 200
9  x

>> 100
>> 200
```

You can also use two variables to perform arithmetic operations:

```
1  # http://tinyurl.com/z8hv5j5
2
3
4  x = 10
5  y = 10
6  z = x + y
7  z
8  a = x - y
9  a

>> 20
>> 0
```

Often when programming, you want to **increment** (increase) or **decrement** (decrease) the value of a variable. Because this is such a standard operation, Python has a special syntax—a shortcut—for incrementing and decrementing variables. To increment a variable, you assign the variable to itself, and on the other side of the equals sign you add the variable to the number you want to increment by:

```
1  # http://tinyurl.com/zvzf786
2
3
4  x = 10
5  x = x + 1
6  x

>> 11
```

To decrement a variable, you do the same thing, but instead subtract the number you want to decrement by:

```
1  # http://tinyurl.com/gmuzdr9
2
3
4  x = 10
5  x = x - 1
6  x
```

>> 9

These examples are perfectly valid, but there is a shorter method you should use instead:

```
1  # http://tinyurl.com/zdva5wq
2
3
4  x = 10
5  x += 1
6  x
```

>> 11

```
1  # http://tinyurl.com/jqw4m5r
2
3
4  x = 10
5  x -= 1
6  x
```

>> 9

Variables are not limited to storing integer values. They can refer to any data type:

```
1  # http://tinyurl.com/jsygqcy
2
3
4  hi = "Hello, World!"
```

```
1 | # http://tinyurl.com/h47ty49
2 |
3 |
4 | my_float = 2.2
```

```
1 | # http://tinyurl.com/hx9xluq
2 |
3 |
4 | my_boolean = True
```

You can name variables whatever you'd like, as long as you follow four rules:

1. Variables can't have spaces. If you want to use two words in a variable, put an underscore between them: i.e., my_variable = "A string!"

2. Variable names can only contain letters, numbers, and the underscore symbol.

3. You cannot start a variable name with a number. Although you can start a variable with an underscore, it has a special meaning that I will cover later, so avoid using it until then.

4. You cannot use Python keywords for variable names. You can find a list of keywords at http://theselftaughtprogrammer.io/keywords.

Syntax

Syntax is the set of rules, principles, and processes that govern the structure of sentences in a given language, specifically word order.[3] The English language has syntax, and so does Python.

In Python, strings are always surrounded by quotes. This is an example of Python's syntax. The following is a valid Python program:

```
1 | # http://tinyurl.com/j7c2npf
2 |
3 |
4 | print("Hello, World!")
```

It is valid because you followed Python's syntax by using quotes around your text when you defined a string. If you only used quotes on one side of your text, you would violate Python's syntax, and your code would not work.

Errors and Exceptions

If you write a Python program and disregard Python's syntax, you will get one or more errors when you run your program. The Python shell will inform you your code did not work, and it will give you information about the error. See what happens if you try to define a string in Python with a quote on only one side:

```
1  # http://tinyurl.com/hp2plhs
2
3
4  # This code has an error.
5
6
7  my_string = "Hello World.
```

```
>> File "/Users/coryalthoff/PycharmProjects/se.py", line 1
my_string = 'd ^ SyntaxError: EOL while scanning string
literal
```

This message tells you there is a **syntax error** in your program. Syntax errors are fatal. A program cannot run with a syntax error. When you try to run a program with a syntax error, Python lets you know about it in the shell. The message tells you what file the error was in, what line it occurred on, and what kind of error it was. Although this error may look intimidating, they happen all the time.

When there is an error in your code, you should go to the line number the problem occurred on and try to figure out what you did wrong. In this example, you would go to the first line of your code. After staring at it for a while, you would eventually notice there is only one quote. To fix the error, add a quote at the end of the string and rerun the program. From this point forward, I will represent the output of an error like this:

```
>> SyntaxError: EOL while scanning string literal
```

For easier reading, I will only show the last line of the error.

Python has two kinds of errors: syntax errors and exceptions. Any error that is not a syntax error is an **exception**. A ZeroDivisionError is an exception that occurs if you try dividing by zero.

Unlike syntax errors, exceptions are not necessarily fatal (there is a way to make a program run even if there is an exception, which you will learn about in the next chapter). When an

exception occurs, Python programmers say "Python (or your program) raised an exception."
Here is an example of an exception:

```
1  # http://tinyurl.com/jxpztcx
2
3
4  # This code has an error.
5
6  10 / 0
```

```
>> ZeroDivisionError: division by zero
```

If you indent your code incorrectly, you get an IndentationError:

```
1  # http://tinyurl.com/gtp6amr
2
3
4  # This code has an error.
5
6
7  y = 2
8          x = 1
```

```
>> IndentationError: unexpected indent
```

As you are learning to program, you will frequently get syntax errors and exceptions (including ones I did not cover), but they will decrease over time. Remember, when you run into a syntax error or exception, go to the line where the problem occurred and look at it and figure out the solution (search the Internet for the error or exception if you are stumped).

Arithmetic Operators

Earlier, you used Python to do simple arithmetic calculations, like 4 / 2. The symbols you used in those examples are called **operators**. Python divides operators into several categories, and the ones you've seen so far are called **arithmetic operators**. Here are some of the most common arithmetic operators in Python:

Operator	Meaning	Example	Evaluates to
**	Exponent	2 ** 2	4
%	Modulo/remainder	14 % 4	2
//	Integer division/floored quotient	13 // 8	1
/	Division	13 / 8	1.625
*	Multiplication	8 * 2	16
-	Subtraction	7 - 1	6
+	Addition	2 + 2	4

When two numbers are divided there is a quotient and a remainder. The quotient is the result of the division, and the remainder is what is left over. The modulo operator returns the remainder. For example, 13 divided by 5 is 2 remainder 3:

```
1  # http://tinyurl.com/grdcl95
2
3
4  13 // 5
```

>> 2

```
1  # http://tinyurl.com/zsqwukd
2
3
4  13 % 5
```

>> 3

When you use modulo with the number two as a divisor, if there is no remainder (modulo returns 0), the number is even. If there is a remainder, the number is odd:

```
1  # http://tinyurl.com/jerpe6u
2
3
4  # even
5  12 % 2
```

>> 0

```
1  # http://tinyurl.com/gkudhcr
2
3
4  # odd
5  11 % 2
```

>> 1

There are two operators used for division. The first is //, which returns the quotient:

```
1  # http://tinyurl.com/hh9fqzy
2
3
4  14 // 3
```

>> 4

The second is /, which returns the result of the first number divided by the second as a floating-point number:

```
1  # http://tinyurl.com/zlkjjdp
2
3
4  14 / 3
```

>> 4.666666666666667

You can raise a number by an exponentiation operator:

```
1  # http://tinyurl.com/h8vuwd4
2
3  2 ** 2
```

>> 4

The values (in this case numbers) on either side of an operator are called **operands**. Together, two operands and an operator form an **expression**. When your program runs, Python evaluates each expression and returns a single value. When you type the expression 2+2 into the shell, Python evaluates it to 4.

The **order of operations** is a set of rules used in mathematical calculations to evaluate an expression. Remember **P**lease **E**xcuse **M**y **D**ear **A**unt **S**ally? It is an acronym to help you remember the order of operations in math equations: parentheses, exponents, multiplication, division, addition, and subtraction. Parentheses outrank exponents, which outrank multiplication and division, which outrank addition and subtraction. If there is a tie among operators, like in the case of $15 / 3 \times 2$, you evaluate from left to right. In this instance, the answer is the result of 15 divided by 3 times 2. Python follows the same order of operations when it evaluates mathematical expressions:

```
1  # http://tinyurl.com/hgjyj7o
2
3
4  2 + 2 * 2
```

```
>> 6
```

```
1  # http://tinyurl.com/hsq7rcz
2
3
4  (2 + 2) * 2
```

```
>> 8
```

In the first example, 2 * 2 is evaluated first because multiplication takes precedence over addition.

In the second example, (2+2) is evaluated first, because Python always evaluates expressions in parentheses first.

Comparison Operators

Comparison operators are another category of operators in Python. Similar to arithmetic operators, they are used in expressions with operands on either side. Unlike expressions with arithmetic operators, expressions with comparison operators evaluate to either True or False.

Operator	Meaning	Example	Evaluates to
>	Greater than	100 > 10	True
<	Less than	100 < 10	False
>=	Greater than or equal to	2 <= 2	True
<=	Less than or equal to	1 <= 4	True
==	Equal	6 == 9	False
!=	Not equal	3 != 2	True

An expression with the > operator returns the value True if the number on the left is greater than the number on the right, and False if it is not:

```
1  # http://tinyurl.com/jm7cxzp
2
3
4  100 > 10
```

>> True

An expression with the < operator returns the value True if the number on the left is less than the number on the right, and False if it is not:

```
1  # http://tinyurl.com/gsdhr8q
2
3
4  100 < 10
```

>> False

An expression with the >= operator returns the value True if the number on the left is greater than or equal to the number on the right. Otherwise, the expression returns False:

```
1  # http://tinyurl.com/jy2oefs
2
3
4  2 >= 2
```

>> True

An expression with the <= operator returns the value True if the number on the left is less than or equal to the number on the right. Otherwise, the expression returns False:

```
1  # http://tinyurl.com/jk599re
2
3
4  2 >= 2
```

>> True

An expression with the == operator returns the value True if the two operands are equal, and False if not:

```
1  # http://tinyurl.com/j2tsz9u
2
3
4  2 == 2
```

> True

```
1
2  # http://tinyurl.com/j5mr2q2
3
4  2 == 3
```

> False

An expression with the != operator returns True if the two operands are not equal, and False otherwise:

```
1  # http://tinyurl.com/gsw3zoe
2
3
4  1 != 2
```

>> True

```
1   # http://tinyurl.com/z7pffk3
2
3
4   2 != 2
```

>> False

Earlier, you assigned variables to numbers, like x = 100, using =. It may be tempting to read this in your head as "x equals 100," but don't. As you saw earlier, = is used to assign a value to a variable, not to check for equality. When you see x = 100, think "x gets one hundred." The comparison operator == is used to test for equality, so if you see x == 100, then think "x equals 100."

Logical Operators

Logical operators are another category of operators in Python. Like comparison operators, logical operators also evaluate to True or False.

Operator	Meaning	Example	Evaluates to
and	and	True and True	True
or	or	True or False	True
not	not	not True	False

The Python keyword and takes two expressions and returns True if all the expressions evaluate to True. If any of the expressions are False, it returns False:

```
1   # http://tinyurl.com/zdqghb2
2
3
4   1 == 1 and 2 == 2
```

>> True

```
1  # http://tinyurl.com/zkp2jzy
2
3
4  1 == 2 and 2 == 2
```

>> False

```
1  # http://tinyurl.com/honkev6
2
3
4  1 == 2 and 2 == 1
```

>> False

```
1  # http://tinyurl.com/zjrxxrc
2
3
4  2 == 1 and 1 == 1
```

>> False

You can use the and keyword multiple times in one statement:

```
1  # http://tinyurl.com/zpvk56u
2
3
4  1 == 1 and 10 != 2 and 2 < 10
```

>> True

The keyword or takes two or more expressions and evaluates to True if any of the expressions evaluate to True:

```
1  # http://tinyurl.com/hosuh7c
2
3
4  1==1 or 1==2
```

>> True

```
1  # http://tinyurl.com/zj6q8h9
2
3
4  1==1 or 2==2
```

>> True

```
1  # http://tinyurl.com/j8ngufo
2
3
4  1==2 or 2==1
```

>> False

```
1  # http://tinyurl.com/z728zxz
2
3
4  2==1 or 1==2
```

>> False

Like and, you can use multiple or keywords in one statement:

```
1  # http://tinyurl.com/ja9mech
2
3
4  1==1 or 1==2 or 1==3
```

>> True

This expression evaluates to True because 1==1 is True, even though the rest of the expressions would evaluate to False.

Placing the keyword not in front of an expression will change the result of the evaluation to the opposite of what it would have otherwise evaluated to. If the expression would have evaluated to True, it will evaluate to False when preceded by not:

```
1 | # http://tinyurl.com/h45eq6v
2 |
3 |
4 | not 1 == 1

>> False

1 | # http://tinyurl.com/gsqj6og
2 |
3 |
4 | not 1 == 2

>> True
```

Conditional Statements

The keywords if, elif, and else are used in **conditional statements**. Conditional statements are a type of **control structure**: a block of code that makes decisions by analyzing the values of variables. A conditional statement is code that can execute additional code conditionally. Here is an example in **pseudocode** (A notation resembling code used to illustrate an example) to clarify how this works:

```
1 | # Do not run
2 |
3 |
4 | If (expression) Then
5 |             (code_area1)
6 | Else
7 |             (code_area2)
```

This pseudocode explains that you can define two conditional statements that work together. If the expression defined in the first conditional statement is True, all the code defined in code_area1 is executed. If the expression defined in the first conditional statement is False, all the code defined in code_area2 is executed. The first part of the example is called an **if-statement**, and the second is called an **else-statement**. Together, they form an **if-else statement**: a way for programmers to say "if this happens do this, otherwise, do that." Here is an example of an if-else statement in Python:

```
1  # http://tinyurl.com/htvy6g3
2
3
4  home = "America"
5  if home == "America":
6      print("Hello, America!")
7  else:
8      print("Hello, World!")
```

>> Hello, America!

Lines 5 and 6 form an if-statement. An if-statement is made up of a line of code starting with the if keyword, followed by an expression, a colon, an indentation, and one or more lines of code to be executed if the expression in the first line evaluates to True. Lines 7 and 8 form an else-statement. An else-statement starts with the else keyword, followed by a colon, an indentation, and one or more lines of code to execute if the expression in the if-statement evaluates to False.

Together they form an if-else statement. This example prints Hello, America!, because the expression in the if-statement evaluates to True. If you change the variable home to Canada, the expression in the if-statement evaluates to False, the else-statement code will execute, and your program will print Hello, World! instead.

```
1  # http://tinyurl.com/jytyg5x
2
3
4  home = "Canada"
5  if home == "America":
6      print("Hello, America!")
7  else:
8      print("Hello, World!")
```

>> Hello, World!

You can use an if-statement by itself:

```
1  # http://tinyurl.com/jyg7dd2
2
3
4  home = "America"
5  if home == "America":
6      print("Hello, America!")
```

>> Hello, America!

You can have multiple if-statements in a row:

```
1   # http://tinyurl.com/z24ckye
2
3
4   x = 2
5   if x == 2:
6       print("The number is 2.")
7   if x % 2 == 0:
8       print("The number is even.")
9   if x % 2 != 0:
10      print("The number is odd.")
```

>> The number is 2.
>> The number is even.

Each if-statement will execute its code only if its expression evaluates to True. In this case, the first two expressions evaluate to True, so their code executes, but the third expression evaluates to False, so its code does not execute.

If you want to get crazy, you can even put an if-statement inside of another if-statement(this is called nesting):

```
1    # http://tinyurl.com/zrodgne
2
3
4    x = 10
5    y = 11
6
7
8    if x == 10:
9        if y == 11:
10            print(x + y)
```

>> 21

In this case, x + y will only print if the expressions in both if-statements evaluate to True. You cannot use an else-statement on its own; they can only be used at the end of an if-else statement.

You can use the elif keyword to create **elif-statements**. elif stands for else if, and elif-statements can be indefinitely added to an if-else statement to allow it to make additional decisions.

If an if-else statement has elif-statements in it, the if-statement expression is evaluated first. If the expression in that statement evaluates to True, only its code is executed. However, if it evaluates to False, each consecutive elif-statement is evaluated. As soon as an expression in an elif-statement evaluates to True, its code is executed and no more code executes. If none of the elif-statements evaluate to True, the code in the else-statement is executed. Here is an example of an if-else statement with elif-statements in it:

```
1   # http://tinyurl.com/jpr265j
2
3
4   home = "Thailand"
5   if home == "Japan":
6       print("Hello, Japan!")
7   elif home == "Thailand":
8       print("Hello, Thailand!")
9   elif home == "India":
10      print("Hello, India!")
11  elif home == "China":
12      print("Hello, China!")
13  else:
14      print("Hello, World!")
```

>> Hello, Thailand!

Here is an example where none of the expressions in the elif-statements evaluate to True, and the code in the else-statement is executed:

```
1   # http://tinyurl.com/zdvuuhs
2
3   home = "Mars"
4   if home == "America":
5       print("Hello, America!")
6   elif home == "Canada":
7       print("Hello, Canada!")
8   elif home == "Thailand":
9       print("Hello, Thailand!")
10  elif home == "Mexico":
11      print("Hello, Mexico!")
12  else:
13      print("Hello, World!")
```

>> Hello, World!

Finally, you can have multiple if-statements and elif-statements in a row:

```
1   # http://tinyurl.com/hzyxgf4
2
3
4   x = 100
5   if x == 10:
6       print("10!")
7   elif x == 20:
8       print("20!")
9   else:
10      print("I don't know!")
11
12
13  if x == 100:
14      print("x is 100!")
15
16
17  if x % 2 == 0:
18      print("x is even!")
19  else:
20      print("x is odd!")
```

```
>> I don't know!
>> x is 100!
>> x is even!
```

Statements

A **statement** is a technical term that describes various parts of the Python language. You can think of a Python statement as a command or calculation. In this section, you will take a detailed look at the syntax of statements. Don't worry if some of this seems confusing at first. It will start making more sense the more time you spend practicing Python and will help you understand several programming concepts.

Python has two kinds of statements: **simple statements** and **compound statements**. Simple statements can be expressed in one line of code, whereas compound statements generally span multiple lines. Here are some examples of simple statements:

```
1   # http://tinyurl.com/jrowero
2
3
4   print("Hello, World!")
```

```
>> Hello, World!
```

```
1  # http://tinyurl.com/h2y549y
2
3
4  2 + 2
```

```
>> 4
```

`if-statements`, `if-else` statements, and the first program you wrote in this chapter that printed `Hello, World!` one hundred times are all examples of compound statements.

Compound statements are made up of one or more **clauses**. A clause consists of two or more lines of code: a **header** followed by a **suite(s)**. A header is a line of code in a clause that contains a keyword, followed by a colon and a sequence of one or more lines of indented code. After the indent, there are one or more suites. A suite is just a line of code in a clause. The header controls the suites. Your program that prints `Hello, World!` a hundred times is made up of a single compound statement:

```
1  # http://tinyurl.com/zfz3eel
2
3  for i in range(100):
4      print("Hello, World!")
```

```
>> Hello, World!
>> Hello, World!
>> Hello, World!
...
```

The first line of the program is the header. It's made up of a keyword—`for`—followed by a colon. After the indentation is a suite—`print("Hello, World!")`. In this case, the header uses the suite to print `Hello, World!` a hundred times. The code in this example is called a loop, which you learn more about in Chapter 7. This code only has one clause.

A compound statement can be made up of multiple clauses. You already saw this with `if-else` statements. Anytime an `if-statement` is followed by an `else-statement`, the result is a compound statement with multiple clauses. When a compound statement has multiple clauses, the header clauses work together. In the case of an `if-`

else compound statement, when the if-statement evaluates to True, the if-statement suites execute, and the else-statement suites do not execute. When the if-statement evaluates to False, the if-statement suites do not execute, but the else-statement suites execute instead. The last example from the previous section includes three compound statements:

```
1   # http://tinyurl.com/hpwkdo4
2
3
4   x = 100
5   if x == 10:
6       print("10!")
7   elif x == 20:
8       print("20!")
9   else:
10      print("I don't know!")
11
12
13  if x == 100:
14      print("x is 100!")
15
16
17  if x % 2 == 0:
18      print("x is even!")
19  else:
20      print("x is odd!")
```

```
>> I don't know!
>> x is 100!
>> x is even!
```

The first compound statement has three clauses; the second compound statement has one clause, and the last compound statement has two clauses.

One last thing about statements, they can have spaces between them. Spaces between statements do not affect the code. Sometimes spaces are used between statements to make code more readable:

```
 1 │ # http://tinyurl.com/zlgcwoc
 2 │
 3 │
 4 │ print("Michael")
 5 │
 6 │
 7 │
 8 │
 9 │
10 │
11 │ print("Jordan")
```

```
>> Michael
>> Jordan
```

Vocabulary

Comment: A line (or part of a line) of code written in English (or another language) preceded by a unique symbol telling the programming language you are using know it should ignore that line (or part of a line) of code.

Keyword: A word with a special meaning in a programming language. You can see all of Python's keywords at http://theselftaughtprogrammer.io/keywords.

Data type: A category of data.

Object: A data value in Python with three properties: an identity, a data type, and a value.

Str: The data type of a string.

String: An object with the data type str. Its value is a sequence of one or more characters surrounded by quotes.

Character: A single symbol like a or 1.

Int: The data type of whole numbers.

Integer: An object with the data type int. Its value is a whole number.

Float: The data type of decimal numbers.

Floating-point number: An object with the data type float. Its value is a decimal number.

Bool: The data type of boolean objects.

Boolean: An object with the data type bool. Its value is either True or False.

NoneType: The data type of None objects.

None: An object with the data type NoneType. Its value is always None.

Constant: A value that never changes.

Variable: A name assigned a value using the assignment operator.

Assignment operator: The = sign in Python.

Increment: Increasing the value of a variable.

Decrement: Decreasing the value of a variable.

Syntax: The set of rules, principles, and processes that govern the structure of sentences in a given language, specifically word order.[4]

Syntax error: A fatal programming error caused by violating a programming language's syntax.

Exception: A nonfatal programming error.

Operator: Symbols used with operands in an expression.

Arithmetic operator: A category of operators used in arithmetic expressions.

Operand: A value on either side of an operator.

Expression: Code with an operator surrounded by two operands.

Order of operations: A set of rules used in mathematical calculations to evaluate an expression.

Comparison operator: A category of operators used in an expression that evaluate to either `True` or `False`.

Logical operator: A category of operators that evaluate two expressions and return either `True` or `False`.

Conditional statement: Code that can execute additional code conditionally.

Control structure: A block of code that makes decisions by analyzing the values of variables.

Pseudocode: A notation resembling code used to illustrate an example.

if-else statement: A way for programmers to say "if this happens do this, otherwise, do that."

if-statement: The first part of an `if-else statement`.

else-statement: The second part of an `if-else statement`.

elif-statement: Statements that can be indefinitely added to an `if-else statement` to allow it to make additional decisions.

Statement: A command or calculation.

Simple statement: A statement that can be expressed in one line of code.

Compound statement: A statement that generally spans multiple lines of code.

Clause: The building blocks of compound statements.
A clause is made up of two or more lines of code: a header followed by a suite(s).

Header: A line of code in a clause containing a keyword, followed by a colon and a sequence of one or more lines of indented code.

Suite: A line of code in a clause controlled by a header.

Challenges

1. Print three different strings.
2. Write a program that prints a message if a variable is less than 10, and different message if the variable is greater than or equal to 10.

3. Write a program that prints a message if a variable is less than or equal to 10, another message if the variable is greater than 10 but less than or equal to 25, and another message if the variable is greater than 25.

4. Create a program that divides two variables and prints the remainder.

5. Create a program that takes two variables, divides them, and prints the quotient.

6. Write a program with a variable age assigned to an integer that prints different strings depending on what integer age is.

Solutions: http://tinyurl.com/zx7o2v9.

Chapter 4. Functions

" Functions should do one thing. They should do it well. They should do it only."
— Robert C. Martin

In this chapter, you will learn about **functions**: compound statements that can take input, execute instructions, and return an output. Functions allow you to define and reuse functionality in your programs.

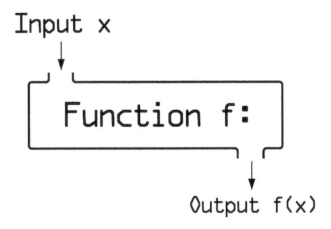

Representing Concepts

From here on out, I will use a new **convention** (an agreed upon way of doing things) to explain programming concepts. Here is an example of the convention I will use: `print("[what_you_want_to_print]")`, which illustrates how to use the print function.

I combined Python code with brackets containing a description to illustrate this concept. When I give an example like this, everything is valid Python code except the brackets and the text inside of them, which need to be replaced with valid code when you follow the example. The text inside the brackets is a hint for what code you should use to replace it. Python uses brackets in its syntax, so I will use double brackets when they should remain in your code.

Functions

Calling a function means giving the function the input it needs to execute its instructions and return an output. Each input to a function is a **parameter**. When you pass a parameter to a function, it is called "passing" the function a parameter.

Functions in Python are similar to mathematical functions. If you don't remember functions from algebra, here is an example:

```
1  # Do not run.
2
3
4
5  f(x) = x * 2
```

The left side of the statement above defines a function, f, that takes one parameter, x. The right side of the statement is the function's definition that uses the parameter passed in (x) to make a calculation and return the result (the output). In this case, the value of the function is defined as the function's parameter value multiplied by two.

In both Python and algebra you invoke a function with the following syntax: [function_name]([parameters_separated_by_commas]). You call a function by putting parentheses after the function name. The parameters go inside the parentheses, with each parameter separated by a comma. For a mathematical function f, defined as f(x) = 2 * x, the value of f(2) is 4, and the value of f(10) is 20.

Defining Functions

To create a function in Python you choose a function name, define its parameters, define what it does, and define what value the function returns. Here is the syntax for defining a function:

```
1  # Do not run.
2
3
4
5  def [function_name]([parameters]):
6      [function_definition]
```

Your mathematical function f(x) = x * 2 looks like this in Python:

```
1  # http://tinyurl.com/j9dctwl
2
3
4  def f(x):
5      return x * 2
```

The keyword def tells Python you are defining a function. After def, you specify the function's name, which must follow the same rules used for variable names. By convention, you should never use capital letters in a function name, and words should be separated by underscores: like_this.

Once you've named your function, put a pair of parentheses after it. Inside the parentheses, define the parameter(s) you want your function to accept.

After the parentheses put a colon and start a new line indented by four spaces (like any other compound statement). Any code indented four spaces after the colon is the function's definition. In this case, the function's definition is only one line—return x * 2. The keyword return defines the value a function outputs when you call it, referred to as the value the function returns.

You can use the syntax [function_name] ([parameters_separated_by_commas]) to call a function in Python. Here is an example of calling a function, f from the previous example, with 2 as a parameter:

```
1  # http://tinyurl.com/zheas3d
2
3
4  # Continue from
5  # last example
6
7
8  f(2)
```

The console didn't print anything. You can save your function's output in a variable and pass it to the print function:

```
1  # http://tinyurl.com/gspjcgj
2
3
4  # Continue from
5  # last example
6
7
8  result = f(2)
9  print(result)
```

>> 4

You can save the result your function returns in a variable whenever you need to use the value later in your program:

```
1   # http://tinyurl.com/znqp8fk
2
3
4   def f(x):
5       return x + 1
6
7
8   z = f(4)
9
10
11  if z == 5:
12      print("z is 5")
13  else:
14      print("z is not 5")
```

```
>> z is 5
```

A function can have one parameter, multiple parameters, or no parameters. To define a function that does not require parameters, leave the parentheses empty when you define your function:

```
1   # http://tinyurl.com/htk7tr6
2
3
4   def f():
5       return 1 + 1
6
7
8   result = f()
9   print(result)
```

```
>> 2
```

If you want your function to accept more than one parameter, you must separate each parameter inside the parentheses with a comma:

```
1  # http://tinyurl.com/gqmkft7
2
3
4  def f(x, y, z):
5      return x + y + z
6
7
8  result = f(1, 2, 3)
9  print(result)
```

>> 6

Finally, a function does not have to include a `return` statement. If a function doesn't have a return statement, it returns `None`:

```
1  # http://tinyurl.com/j8qyqov
2
3
4  def f():
5      z = 1 + 1
6
7
8  result = f()
9  print(result)
```

>> None

Built-In Functions

Python comes with a library of functions built into the programming language called **built-in functions**. They perform all sorts of different computations and tasks and are ready to use without any work on your part. You've already seen one example of a built-in function: the first program you wrote used the `print` function to print `"Hello, World!"`.

`len` is another built-in function. It returns the length of an object—for example, the length of a string (the number of characters in it):

```
1  # http://tinyurl.com/zfkzqw6
2
3
4  len("Monty")
```

```
>> 5
```

```
1  # http://tinyurl.com/h75c3cf
2
3
4  len("Python")
```

```
>> 6
```

The built-in str function takes an object and returns a new object with a str data type. For example, you can use str to convert an integer to a string:

```
1  # http://tinyurl.com/juzxg2z
2
3
4  str(100)
```

```
>> '100'
```

The int function takes an object and returns an integer object:

```
1  # http://tinyurl.com/j42qhkf
2
3
4  int("1")
```

```
>> 1
```

The float function takes an object and returns a floating-point number object:

```
1  # http://tinyurl.com/hnk8gh2
2
3
4  float(100)
```

```
>> 100.0
```

The parameter you pass to a str, int, or float function must be able to become a string, integer, or a floating-point number. The str function can accept most objects a parameter, but the int function can only accept a string with a number in it or a floating-point object.

The float function can only take a string with a number in it or an integer object:

```
1  # http://tinyurl.com/jcchmlx
2
3
4  int("110")
5  int(20.54)
6
7
8  float("16.4")
9  float(99)
```

```
>> 110
>> 20
>> 16.4
>> 99.0
```

Python will raise an exception if you try to pass the int or float function a parameter it cannot convert to an integer or a floating-point number:

```
1  # http://tinyurl.com/zseo2ls
2
3
4  int("Prince")
```

```
>> ValueError: invalid literal for int() with base 10:
'Prince'
```

input is a built-in function that collects information from the person using the program:

```
1  # http://tinyurl.com/zynprpg
2
3
4  age = input("Enter your age:")
5  int_age = int(age)
6  if int_age < 21:
7      print("You are young!")
8  else:
9      print("Wow, you are old!")
```

```
>> Enter your age:
```

The `input` function takes a string as a parameter and displays it to the person using the program in the shell. The user can then type a response into the shell, and you can save their response in a variable—in this case, to the variable `age`.

Next, use the `int` function to change the variable `age` from a string to an integer. The `input` function collects data from the user as a `str`, but you want your variable to be an `int` so you can compare it to other integers. Once you have an integer, your `if-else` `statement` determines which message prints for the user, depending on what they typed into the shell. If the user types a number less than 21, You are young! prints. If the user types a number greater than 21, Wow, you are old! prints.

Reusing Functions

Functions are not only used to compute and return values. Functions can encapsulate functionality you want to reuse:

```
1   # http://tinyurl.com/zhy8y4m
2
3
4   def even_odd(x):
5       if x % 2 == 0:
6           print("even")
7       else:
8           print("odd")
9
10
11  even_odd(2)
12  even_odd(3)
```

```
>> even
>> odd
```

You didn't define a value for your function to return, but your function is still useful. It tests if `x % 2 == 0`, and prints whether x is even or odd.

Functions allow you to write less code because you can reuse functionality. Here is an example of a program written without functions:

```
1   # http://tinyurl.com/jk8lugl
2
3
4   n = input("type a number:")
5   n = int(n)
6
7
8   if n % 2 == 0:
9       print("n is even.")
10  else:
11      print("n is odd.")
12
13
14  n = input("type a number:")
15  n = int(n)
16  if n % 2 == 0:
17      print("n is even.")
18  else:
19      print("n is odd.")
20
21
22  n = input("type a number:")
23  n = int(n)
24  if n % 2 == 0:
25      print("n is even.")
26  else:
27      print("n is odd.")
```

```
>> type a number:
```

This program asks the user to enter a number three times. Then, an if-else statement checks if the number is even. If it is, n is even. prints, otherwise n is odd. prints.

The problem with the program is it repeats the same code three times. You can make this program shorter and easier to read by putting your functionality in a function and calling it three times:

```
 1   # http://tinyurl.com/zzn22mz
 2
 3
 4   def even_odd():
 5       n = input("type a number:")
 6       n = int(n)
 7       if n % 2 == 0:
 8           print("n is even.")
 9       else:
10           print("n is odd.")
11
12
13   even_odd()
14   even_odd()
15   even_odd()
```

```
>> type a number:
```

This new program has the same functionality as your previous program, but because you put your functionality in a function you can call whenever needed, your program is much shorter and easier to read.

Required and Optional Parameters

There are two types of parameters a function can accept. The parameters you've seen so far are called **required parameters**. When a user calls a function, they must pass all of the required parameters into it, or Python will raise an exception.

Python has another kind of parameter—**optional parameters**—that let the caller of the function pass in a parameter if necessary, but it is not required. If an optional parameter is not passed in, the function will use its default value instead. Optional parameters are defined with the following syntax: [function_name] ([parameter_name]= [parameter_ value]). Like required parameters, optional parameters must be separated by commas. Here is an example of a function that takes an optional parameter:

```
1  # http://tinyurl.com/h3ych4h
2
3
4  def f(x=2):
5      return x**x
6
7
8  print(f())
9  print(f(4))

>> 4
>> 256
```

First, you call your function without passing in a parameter. Because the parameter is optional, x automatically gets 2 and the function returns 4.

Next, you call your function and pass in 4 as a parameter. The function ignores the default value, x gets 4 and the function returns 256. You can define a function that has both required and optional parameters, but you must define all the required parameters before the optional ones:

```
1  # http://tinyurl.com/hm5svn9
2
3
4  def add_it(x, y=10):
5      return x + y
6
7
8  result = add_it(2)
9  print(result)

>> 12
```

Scope

Variables have an important property called **scope**. When you define a variable, its scope refers to what part of your program can read and write to it. Reading a variable means finding its value. Writing a variable means changing its value. A variable's scope is determined by where in your program it is defined. If you define a variable outside of a function (or class, which you learn about in Part II), the variable has a **global scope**: It can be read or written to from anywhere in your program. A variable with global scope is called a **global variable**. If you define a variable inside of a function (or class), it has **local scope**: your program can only read or write to it in the function (or class) the variable was defined within. Here are variables with global scope:

```
1   # http://tinyurl.com/zhmxnqt
2
3
4   x = 1
5   y = 2
6   z = 3
```

These variables were not defined inside of a function (or class), and therefore have a global scope. This means you can read or write to them from anywhere—including inside of a function:

```
1    # http://tinyurl.com/hgvnj4p
2
3
4    x = 1
5    y = 2
6    z = 3
7
8
9    def f():
10       print(x)
11       print(y)
12       print(z)
13
14
15   f()
```

```
>> 1
>> 2
>> 3
```

If you define these same variables inside of a function, you can only read or write to them from inside of that function. If you try to access them outside of the function they were defined in Python raises an exception:

```
1   # http://tinyurl.com/znka93k
2
3
4   def f():
5       x = 1
6       y = 2
7       z = 3
8
9
10  print(x)
11  print(y)
12  print(z)
```

>> NameError: name 'x' is not defined

If you define variables inside your function, your code works:

```
1   # http://tinyurl.com/z2k3jds
2
3
4   def f():
5       x = 1
6       y = 2
7       z = 3
8       print(x)
9       print(y)
10      print(z)
11
12
13  f()
```

>> 1
>> 2
>> 3

Trying to use a variable defined inside of a function outside of it is similar to using a variable that hasn't been defined yet, which will cause Python to raise the same exception:

```
1  # http://tinyurl.com/zn8zjmr
2
3
4  if x > 100:
5      print("x is > 100")
```

```
>> NameError: name 'x' is not defined
```

You can write to a global variable from anywhere, but writing to a global variable inside of a local scope takes an extra step. You must explicitly use the `global` keyword, followed by the variable you want to change. Python makes you take this extra step to ensure that if you define the variable x inside of a function, you will not accidentally change the value of any previously defined variables outside of your function. Here is an example of writing to a global variable from inside a function:

```
1   # http://tinyurl.com/zclmda7
2
3
4   x = 100
5
6
7   def f():
8       global x
9       x += 1
10      print(x)
11
12
13  f()
```

```
>> 101
```

Without scope, you could access every variable anywhere in your program, which would be problematic. If you have a large program, and you write a function that uses the variable x, you might accidently change the value of a variable also called x that you previously defined elsewhere in your program. Mistakes like that can alter the behavior of your program and may cause errors or unexpected results. The larger your program gets, and the more variables it has, the more likely this becomes.

Exception Handling

Relying on user input from the `input` function means you do not control the input to your program—the user does, and that input could cause an error. For example, say you write a program that collects two numbers from a user and prints the result of the first number divided by the second number:

```
1  # http://tinyurl.com/jcg5qwp
2
3
4  a = input("type a number:")
5  b = input("type another:")
6  a = int(a)
7  b = int(b)
8  print(a / b)
```

```
>> type a number:
>> 10
>> type another:
>> 5
>> 2
```

Your program appears to work. However, you will run into a problem if the user inputs 0 as the second number:

```
1  # http://tinyurl.com/ztpcjs4
2
3
4  a = input("type a number:")
5  b = input("type another:")
6  a = int(a)
7  b = int(b)
8  print(a / b)
```

```
>> type a number:
>> 10
>> type another:
>> 0
>> ZeroDivisionError: integer division or modulo by zero
```

You cannot just hope someone using this program will not enter 0 as the second number.

One way to solve this is to use **exception handling**, which allows you to test for error conditions, "catch" exceptions if they occur, and decide how to proceed.

The keywords `try` and `except` are used for exception handling. When you change this program to use exception handling, if a user enters 0 as the second number, instead of raising an exception, the program could print a message telling them not to enter 0.

Each exception in Python is an object, so you can use them in your programs. You can see a list of built-in exceptions here: https://www.tutorialspoint.com/python/standard_exceptions.htm. If you are in a situation where you think your code may raise an exception, use a compound statement with the keywords `try` and `except` to catch it.

The `try` clause contains the error that could occur. The `except` clause contains code that will only execute if the exception in your `try` clause occurs. Here is an example of how you can use exception handling in your program, so if a user enters 0 as the second number, your program doesn't break:

```
1   # http://tinyurl.com/j2scn4f
2
3
4   a = input("type a number:")
5   b = input("type another:")
6   a = int(a)
7   b = int(b)
8   try:
9       print(a / b)
10  except ZeroDivisionError:
11      print("b cannot be zero.")
```

```
>> type a number:
>> 10
>> type another:
>> 0
>> b cannot be zero.
```

If the user enters anything other than 0 for b, the code in the `try` block executes, and the `except` block doesn't do anything. If the user enters 0 for b, instead of raising an exception, the code in your `except` block is executed and your program prints b cannot be zero.

Your program will also break if the user enters a string that Python cannot convert to an integer:

```
1  a = input("type a number:")
2  b = input("type another:")
3  a = int(a)
4  b = int(b)
5  try:
6      print(a / b)
7  except ZeroDivisionError:
8      print("b cannot be zero.")
```

```
>> type a number:
>> Hundo
>> type another:
>> Million
>> ValueError: invalid literal for int() with base 10:
'Hundo'
```

You can fix this by moving the part of your program that collects input inside of your try statement, and telling your except statement to look out for two exceptions: a ZeroDivisionError and a ValueError. A ValueError occurs if you give the built-in functions int, string, or float bad input. You can have your except statement catch two exceptions by adding parentheses around except and separating the exceptions with a comma:

```
1  # http://tinyurl.com/jlus42v
2
3
4  try:
5      a = input("type a number:")
6      b = input("type another:")
7      a = int(a)
8      b = int(b)
9      print(a / b)
10 except (ZeroDivisionError,
11         ValueError):
12     print("Invalid input.")
```

```
>> type a number:
>> Hundo
>> type another:
>> Million
>> Invalid input.
```

Don't use variables defined in a `try` statement in an `except` statement, because an exception could occur before the variable is defined, and an exception will get raised inside of your `except` statement when you try to use it:

```
1   # http://tinyurl.com/hockur5
2
3
4   try:
5       10 / 0
6       c = "I will never get defined."
7   except ZeroDivisionError:
8       print(c)
```

```
>> NameError: name 'c' is not defined
```

Docstrings

When you define a function with parameters, sometimes the parameters have to be a particular data type for the function to work. How do you communicate this to whoever calls your function? When you write a function, it is good practice to leave a comment called a **docstring** at the top of the function explaining what data type each parameter needs to be. Docstrings explain what the function does, and document what kinds of parameters it needs:

```
1    # http://tinyurl.com/zhahdcg
2
3
4    def add(x, y):
5        """
6        Returns x + y.
7        :param x: int.
8        :param y: int.
9        :return: int sum of x and y.
10       """
11       return x + y
```

The first line of the docstring clearly explains what your function does, so when other developers reuse your function or method, they do not have to read through all of your code to figure out its purpose. The rest of the docstring's lines list the function's parameters, the parameter types, and what it returns. Docstrings will help you program faster because you can read a docstring to figure out what a function does, instead of reading all the code.

To keep the examples in this book concise, I've omitted docstrings I would usually include. Normally when I write code, I include docstrings to make my code easy to understand for everyone who reads it in the future.

Only Use a Variable When Needed

Only save data in a variable if you are going to use it later. For example, do not store an integer in a variable just to print it:

```
1  # http://tinyurl.com/zptktex
2
3
4  x = 100
5  print(x)
```

>> 100

Instead, pass the integer directly to the print function:

```
1  # http://tinyurl.com/hmwr4kd
2
3
4  print(100)
```

>> 100

I violate this rule in many examples in this book to make what I'm doing easy for you to understand. You don't need to do the same when you are writing code.

Vocabulary

Functions: Compound statements that can take input, execute instructions, and return an output.
Convention: An agreed upon way of doing things.
Calling: Giving the function the input it needs to execute its instructions and return an output.
Parameter: Data passed into a function.
Required parameter: A non-optional parameter.
Optional parameter: An optional parameter.
Built-in function: A function that comes with Python.
Scope: Where a variable can be read or written to.

Global scope: The scope of a variable that can be read or written to from anywhere in a program.

Global variable: A variable with a global scope.

Local scope: The scope of a variable that can only be read or written to from the function (or class) the variable was defined within.

Exception handling: A programming concept that allows you to test for error conditions, "catch" exceptions if they occur, and decide how to proceed.

Docstring: Docstrings explain what a function does, and documents what kinds of parameters it takes.

Challenges

1. Write a function that takes a number as an input and returns that number squared.
2. Create a function that accepts a string as a parameter and prints it.
3. Write a function that takes three required parameters and two optional parameters.
4. Write a program with two functions. The first function should take an integer as a parameter and return the result of the integer divided by 2. The second function should take an integer as a parameter and return the result of the integer multiplied by 4. Call the first function, save the result as a variable, and pass it as a parameter to the second function.
5. Write a function that converts a string to a `float` and returns the result. Use exception handling to catch the exception that could occur.
6. Add a docstring to all of the functions you wrote in challenges 1-5.

Solutions: http://tinyurl.com/hkzgqrv.

Chapter 5. Containers

"The fool wonders, the wise man asks."
— Benjamin Disraeli

In Chapter 3, you learned how to store objects in variables. In this chapter, you find out how to store objects in containers. Containers are like filing cabinets: they keep your data organized. You will learn three commonly used containers: lists, tuples, and dictionaries.

Methods

In Chapter 4, you learned about functions. Python has a similar concept called **methods**. Methods are functions closely associated with a given type of data. Methods execute code and can return a result just like a function. Unlike a function, you call a method on an object. You can also pass them parameters. Here is an example of calling the methods `upper` and `replace` on a string:

```
1  # http://tinyurl.com/zdllght
2
3
4  "Hello".upper()
```

```
>> 'HELLO'
```

```
1  # http://tinyurl.com/hfgpst5
2
3
4  "Hello".replace("o", "@")
```

```
>> 'Hell@'
```

You will learn more about methods in Part II.

Lists

A **list** is a container that stores objects in a specific order.

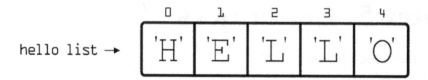

Lists are represented with brackets. There are two syntaxes you can use to create a list. You can create an empty list with the `list` function:

```
1   # http://tinyurl.com/h4go6kg
2
3
4   fruit = list()
5   fruit
```

```
>> []
```

Or, with brackets:

```
1   # http://tinyurl.com/jft8p7x
2
3
4   fruit = []
5   fruit
```

```
>> []
```

You can create a list with items already in it by using the second syntax `[]`, and placing each item you want in the list inside the brackets, separated by commas:

```
1   # http://tinyurl.com/h2y8nos
2
3
4   fruit = ["Apple", "Orange", "Pear"]
5   fruit
```

```
>> ['Apple', 'Orange', 'Pear']
```

There are three items in your list: `"Apple"`, `"Orange"`, and `"Pear"`. Lists store items in order. Unless you change the order of your list, `"Apple"` will always be the first item, `"Orange"` the second, and `"Pear"` the third. `"Apple"` is at the beginning of the list, and

"Pear" is at the end. Add a new item to a list using the append method:

```
1  # http://tinyurl.com/h9w3z2m
2
3
4  fruit = ["Apple", "Orange", "Pear"]
5  fruit.append("Banana")
6  fruit.append("Peach")
7  fruit
```

>> ['Apple', 'Orange', 'Pear', 'Banana', 'Peach']

Each object passed to the append method is now an item in your list. append always adds a new item to the end of the list.

Lists are not limited to storing strings—they can store any data type:

```
1  # http://tinyurl.com/zhpntsr
2
3
4  random = []
5  random.append(True)
6  random.append(100)
7  random.append(1.1)
8  random.append("Hello")
9  random
```

>> [True, 100, 1.1, 'Hello']

Strings, lists and tuples are **iterable**. An object is iterable when you can access each item using a loop. Objects that are iterable are called **iterables**. Each item in an iterable has an **index**—a number representing the item's position in the iterable. The first item in a list has an index of 0, not 1.

In the following example, "Apple" is at index 0, "Orange" is at index 1, and "Pear" is at index 2:

```
1  # http://tinyurl.com/z8zzk8d
2
3
4  fruit = ["Apple", "Orange", "Pear"]
```

You can retrieve an item with its index using the syntax [list_name][[index]]:

```
1  # http://tinyurl.com/jqtlwpf
2
3
4  fruit = ["Apple", "Orange", "Pear"]
5  fruit[0]
6  fruit[1]
7  fruit[2]
```

```
>> 'Apple'
>> 'Orange'
>> 'Pear'
```

If you try to access an index that doesn't exist, Python raises an exception:

```
1  # http://tinyurl.com/za3rv95
2
3
4  colors = ["blue", "green", "yellow"]
5  colors[4]
```

```
>> IndexError: list index out of range
```

Lists are **mutable**. When a container is mutable, you can add or remove objects from the container. You can change an item in a list by assigning its index to a new object:

```
1  # http://tinyurl.com/h4ahvf9
2
3
4  colors = ["blue", "green", "yellow"]
5  colors
6  colors[2] = "red"
7  colors
```

```
>> ['blue', 'green', 'yellow']
>> ['blue', 'green', 'red']
```

You can remove the last item from a list using the method pop:

```
1   # http://tinyurl.com/j52uvmq
2
3
4   colors = ["blue", "green", "yellow"]
5   colors
6   item = colors.pop()
7   item
8   colors
```

```
>> ['blue', 'green', 'yellow']
>> 'yellow'
>> ['blue', 'green']
```

You cannot use pop on an empty list. If you try to, Python will raise an exception.

You can combine two lists with the addition operator:

```
1   http://tinyurl.com/jjxnk4z
2
3
4   colors1 = ["blue", "green", "yellow"]
5   colors2 = ["orange", "pink", "black"]
6   colors1 + colors2
```

```
>> ['blue', 'green', 'yellow', 'orange', pink, 'black']
```

You can check if an item is in a list with the keyword in:

```
1   # http://tinyurl.com/z4fnv39
2
3
4   colors = ["blue", "green"," yellow"]
5   "green" in colors
```

```
>> True
```

Use the keyword not to check if an item is not in a list:

```
1 | # http://tinyurl.com/jqzk8pj
2 |
3 |
4 | colors = ["blue", "green", "yellow"]
5 | "black" not in colors
```

>> True

You can get the size of a list (the number of items in it) with the len function:

```
1 | # http://tinyurl.com/hhx6rx4
2 |
3 |
4 | len(colors)
```

>> 3

Here is an example of how you might use a list in practice:

```
 1 | # http://tinyurl.com/gq7yjr7
 2 |
 3 |
 4 | colors = ["purple",
 5 |            "orange",
 6 |            "green"]
 7 |
 8 |
 9 | guess = input("Guess a color:")
10 |
11 |
12 | if guess in colors:
13 |     print("You guessed correctly!")
14 | else:
15 |     print("Wrong! Try again.")
```

>> Guess a color:

Your colors list contains different strings representing colors. Your program uses the built-in input function to ask the user to guess a color, and you save their answer in a variable. If their answer is in the colors list, your program lets the user know they guessed correctly. Otherwise, it prompts them to guess again.

Tuples

A **tuple** is a container that stores objects in a specific order. Unlike lists, tuples are **immutable**, which means their contents cannot change. Once you create a tuple, you cannot modify the value of any of the items in it, add new items to it, or remove items from it. You represent tuples with parentheses. You must separate items in a tuple with commas. There are two syntaxes to create a tuple:

```
1  # http://tinyurl.com/zo88eal
2
3
4  my_tuple = tuple()
5  my_tuple
```

>> ()

And:

```
1  # http://tinyurl.com/zm3y26j
2
3
4  my_tuple = ()
5  my_tuple
```

>> ()

To add objects to a tuple, create one with the second syntax with each item you want to add, separating them with commas:

```
1  # http://tinyurl.com/zlwwfe3
2
3
4  rndm = ("M. Jackson", 1958, True)
5  rndm
```

>> ('M. Jackson', 1958, True)

Even if a tuple only has one item in it, you need to put a comma after it. That way, Python can differentiate it from a number surrounded by parentheses that denote its position in the order of operations:

```
1  # http://tinyurl.com/j8mca8o
2
3
4  # this is a tuple
5  ("self_taught",)
6
7
8  # this is not a tuple
9  (9) + 1
```

```
>> ('self_taught',)
>> 10
```

You cannot add new items to a tuple or change it once you've created it. If you try to change an object in a tuple after you've created it, Python will raise an exception:

```
1  # http://tinyurl.com/z3x34nk
2
3
4  dys = ("1984",
5         "Brave New World",
6         "Fahrenheit 451")
7
8
9  dys[1] = "Handmaid's Tale"
```

```
>> TypeError: 'tuple' object does not support item assignment
```

You can get items from a tuple the same way you would from a list—by referencing the item's index:

```
1  # http://tinyurl.com/z9dc6lo
2
3
4  dys = ("1984",
5         "Brave New World",
6         "Fahrenheit 451")
7
8
9  dys[2]
```

```
>> 'Fahrenheit 451'
```

You can check if an item is in a tuple using the keyword `in`:

```
1  # http://tinyurl.com/j3bsel7
2
3
4  dys = ("1984",
5        "Brave New World",
6        "Fahrenheit 451")
7
8
9  "1984" in dys
```

```
>> True
```

Put the keyword `not` before `in` to check if an item is not in a tuple:

```
1  # http://tinyurl.com/jpdjjv9
2
3
4  dys = ("1984",
5        "Brave New World",
6        "Fahrenheit 451")
7
8
9  "Handmaid's Tale" not in dys
```

```
>> True
```

You may be wondering why you would want to use a data structure that appears to be a less flexible list. Tuples are useful when you are dealing with values you know will never change, and you want to ensure other parts of your program won't change them. Geographic coordinates are an example of data that is useful to store in a tuple. You should store the longitude and latitude of a city in a tuple because those values are never going to change and storing the data in a tuple ensures other parts of your program can't accidentally change them. Tuples—unlike lists—can be used as keys in dictionaries, which you will learn about in the next section of this chapter.

Dictionaries

Dictionaries are another built-in container for storing objects. They are used to link one object, called a **key**, to another object—called the **value**. Linking one object to another is called **mapping**. The result is a **key-value pair**. You add key-value pairs to a dictionary. You can then look up a key in the dictionary and get its value. You cannot, however, use a value to look up a key.

Dictionaries are mutable, so you can add new key-value pairs to them. Unlike lists and tuples, dictionaries do not store objects in a specific order. Their usefulness relies on the associations formed between keys and values, and there are many situations where you need to store data in pairs. For example, you could store information about someone in a dictionary. You could map a key called height to a value representing the person's height, a key called eyecolor to a value representing the person's eye color and a key called nationality to a value representing the person's nationality.

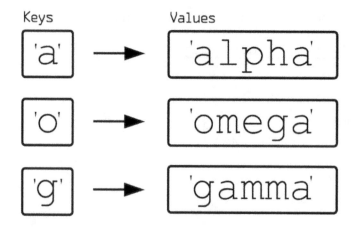

Dictionaries are represented with curly brackets. There are two syntaxes for creating dictionaries:

```
1  # http://tinyurl.com/zfn6jmw
2
3
4  my_dict = dict()
5  my_dict
```

```
>> {}
```

And:

```
1  # http://tinyurl.com/jfgemf2
2
3
4  my_dict = {}
5  my_dict
```

>> {}

You can add key-value pairs to a dictionary when you create it. The first syntax has the key separated from the value by an assignment operator, and the second has the key separated from the value by a colon. A comma must separate each key-value pair. Unlike a tuple, if you have just one key-value pair, you do not need a comma after it. Here is how you add key-value pairs to a dictionary when you create it:

```
1  # http://tinyurl.com/hplqc4u
2
3
4  fruits = {"Apple":
5           "Red",
6           "Banana":
7           "Yellow"}
8  fruits
```

>> {'Apple': 'Red', 'Banana': 'Yellow'}

Your shell output might list the dictionary items in a different order than this example because dictionaries do not store their keys in order, and Python prints the items in an arbitrary order (this applies to all the examples in this section).

Dictionaries are mutable. Once you've created a dictionary, you can add key-value pairs to it with the syntax [dictionary_name][[key]]=[value], and look up a value using a key with the syntax [dictionary_name][key]:

```
 1  # http://tinyurl.com/grc28lh
 2
 3
 4  facts = dict()
 5
 6
 7  # add a value
 8  facts["code"] = "fun"
 9  # look up a key
10  facts["code"]
11
12
13  # add a value
14  facts["Bill"] = "Gates"
15  # look up a key
16  facts["Bill"]
17
18
19  # add a value
20  facts["founded"] = 1776
21  # look up a key
22  facts["founded"]
```

```
>> 'fun'
>> Gates
>> 1776
```

Any object can be a dictionary value. In the previous example, the first two values are strings, and the last value, 1776, is an integer.

Unlike a dictionary value, a dictionary key must be immutable. A string or a tuple can be a dictionary key, but not a list or a dictionary.

Use the in keyword to check if a key is in a dictionary. You cannot use the in keyword to check if a value is in a dictionary:

```
1   # http://tinyurl.com/hgf9vmp
2
3
4   bill = {"Bill Gates":
5           "charitable"}
6
7
8   "Bill Gates" in bill

>> True
```

If you try to access a key that isn't in a dictionary, Python will raise an exception.

Add the keyword not to in to check if a key is not in a dictionary:

```
1   # http://tinyurl.com/he3g993
2
3
4   bill = {"Bill Gates":
5           "charitable"}
6
7
8   "Bill Doors" not in bill

>> True
```

You can delete a key-value pair from a dictionary with the keyword del:

```
1   # http://tinyurl.com/htrd9lj
2
3
4   books = {"Dracula": "Stoker",
5           "1984": "Orwell",
6           "The Trial": "Kafka"}
7
8
9   del books["The Trial"]
10
11  books

>> {'Dracula': 'Stoker', "1984": 'Orwell'}
```

Here is an example of a program using a dictionary:

```
1   # http://tinyurl.com/gnjvep7
2
3
4   rhymes = {"1": "fun",
5             "2": "blue",
6             "3": "me",
7             "4": "floor",
8             "5": "live"
9             }
10
11
12  n = input("Type a number:")
13  if n in rhymes:
14      rhyme = rhymes[n]
15      print(rhyme)
16  else:
17      print("Not found.")
```

>> Type a number:

Your dictionary (rhymes) has six song names (keys) mapped to six musicians (values). You ask the user to type the name of a song and save their response in a variable. Before you look up their response in your dictionary, check to make sure the key exists using the in keyword. If the key exists, you look up the name of the song in your dictionary and print the name of the artist who sings it. Otherwise, you print a message letting the user know the name of the song is not available.

Containers in Containers

You can store containers in other containers. For example, you can store lists in a list:

```
 1  # http://tinyurl.com/gops9fz
 2
 3
 4  lists = []
 5  rap = ["Kanye West",
 6          "Jay Z",
 7          "Eminem",
 8          "Nas"]
 9
10
11  rock = ["Bob Dylan",
12           "The Beatles",
13           "Led Zeppelin"]
14
15
16  djs = ["Zeds Dead",
17          "Tiesto"]
18
19
20  lists.append(rap)
21  lists.append(rock)
22  lists.append(djs)
23
24
25  print(lists)
```

```
>> [['Kanye West', 'Jay Z', 'Eminem', 'Nas'],
['Bob Dylan', 'The Beatles', 'Led Zeppelin'],
['Zeds Dead', 'Tiesto']]
```

In this example, lists has three indexes. Each index is a list: the first index is a list of rappers, the second index is a list of rockers, and the third index is a list of DJs. You can access these lists using their corresponding index:

```
1   # http://tinyurl.com/gu4mudk
2
3
4   # Continue from
5   # last example
6
7   rap = lists[0]
8   print(rap)
```

>> ['Kanye West', 'Jay Z', 'Eminem', 'Nas']

If you append a new item to your rap list, you will see the change when you print your lists:

```
 1   # http://tinyurl.com/hdtosm2
 2
 3
 4   # Continue from
 5   # last example
 6
 7
 8   rap = lists[0]
 9   rap.append("Kendrick Lamar")
10   print(rap)
11   print(lists)
```

>> ['Kanye West', 'Jay Z', 'Eminem', 'Nas', 'Kendrick Lamar']
>> [['Kanye West', 'Jay Z', 'Eminem', 'Nas', 'Kendrick Lamar'],
['Bob Dylan', 'The Beatles', 'Led Zeppelin'], ['Zeds Dead',
'Tiesto']]

You can store a tuple inside a list, a list inside a tuple, and a dictionary inside of a list or a tuple:

```
1  # http://tinyurl.com/z9dhema
2
3
4  locations = []
5
6
7  la = (34.0522, 188.2437)
8  chicago = (41.8781, 87.6298)
9
10
11  locations.append(la)
12  locations.append(chicago)
13
14
15  print(locations)
```

>> [(34.0522, 188.2437), (41.8781, 87.6298)]

```
1  # http://tinyurl.com/ht7gpsd
2
3
4  eights = ["Edgar Allan Poe",
5            "Charles Dickens"]
6
7
8  nines = ["Hemingway",
9           "Fitzgerald",
10          "Orwell"]
11
12
13  authors = (eights, nines)
14  print(authors)
```

>> (['Edgar Allan Poe', 'Charles Dickens'], ['Hemingway', 'Fitzgerald', 'Orwell'])

```
1   # http://tinyurl.com/h8ck5er
2
3
4   bday = {"Hemingway":
5           "7.21.1899",
6           "Fitzgerald":
7           "9.24.1896"}
8
9
10  my_list = [bday]
11  print(my_list)
12  my_tuple = (bday,)
13  print(my_tuple)
```

```
>> [{'Hemingway': '7.21.1899', 'Fitzgerald': '9.24.1896'}]
>> ({'Hemingway': '7.21.1899', 'Fitzgerald': '9.24.1896'},)
```

A list, tuple, or dictionary can be a value in a dictionary:

```
1   # http://tinyurl.com/zqupwx4
2
3
4   ny = {"location":
5         (40.7128,
6          74.0059),
7
8
9         "celebs":
10        ["W. Allen",
11         "Jay Z",
12         "K. Bacon"],
13
14        "facts":
15        {"state":
16         "NY",
17         "country":
18         "America"}
19  }
```

In this example, your dictionary, ny, has three keys: "location", "celebs", and "facts". The first key's value is a tuple because geographic coordinates never change.

The second key's value is a list of celebrities that live in New York, and it is a list because this could change. The third key's value is a dictionary because key-value pairs are the best way to present facts about New York.

Vocabulary

Method: Functions closely associated with a given type of data.
List: A container that stores objects in a specific order.
Iterable: An object is iterable when you can access each item using a loop.
Iterables: Objects that are iterable like strings, lists, and tuples.
Index: A number representing a position in an iterable.
Mutable: When a container is mutable the contents of the container can change.
Immutable: When a container is immutable the contents of the container cannot change.
Dictionary: A built-in container for storing objects used to map one object—called a key —to another object—called the value.
Key: A value used to look up a value in a dictionary.
Value: A value mapped to a key in a dictionary.
Mapping: Linking one object to another.
Key-value pair: A key mapped to a value in a dictionary.

Challenges

1. Create a list of your favorite musicians.
2. Create a list of tuples, with each tuple containing the longitude and latitude of somewhere you've lived or visited.
3. Create a dictionary that contains different attributes about you: height, favorite color, favorite author, etc.
4. Write a program that lets the user ask your height, favorite color, or favorite author, and returns the result from the dictionary you created in the previous challenge.
5. Create a dictionary mapping your favorite musicians to a list of your favorite songs by them.
6. Lists, tuples, and dictionaries are just a few of the containers built into Python. Research Python sets (a type of container). When would you use a set?

Solutions: http://tinyurl.com/z54w9cb.

Chapter 6. String Manipulation

"In theory, there is no difference between theory and practice. But, in practice, there is."
—Jan L. A. van de Snepscheut

Python has built-in functionality for manipulating strings, such as splitting a string into two parts at a given character or changing a string's case. For example, if you have a string IN ALL CAPS, and you want it to be all lowercase, you can change its case using Python. In this chapter, you will learn more about strings and go over some of Python's most useful tools for manipulating them.

Triple Strings

If a string spans more than one line, you have to put it in triple quotes:

```
1   # http://tinyurl.com/h59ygda
2
3
4   """ line one
5       line two
6       line three
7   """
```

If you try to define a string that spans more than one line with single or double quotes, you will get a syntax error.

Indexes

Strings, like lists and tuples, are iterable. You can look up each character in a string with an index. Like other iterables, the first character in a string is at index 0, and each subsequent index is incremented by 1:

```
1  # http://tinyurl.com/zqqc2jw
2
3
4  author = "Kafka"
5  author[0]
6  author[1]
7  author[2]
8  author[3]
9  author[4]
```

```
>> 'K'
>> 'a'
>> 'f'
>> 'k'
>> 'a'
```

In this example, you used the indexes 0, 1, 2, 3, and 4 to look up each of the characters in the string "Kafka". If you try to look up a character past the last index in your string, Python raises an exception:

```
1  # http://tinyurl.com/zk52tef
2
3
4  author = "Kafka"
5  author[5]
```

```
>> IndexError: string index out of range
```

Python also allows you to look up each item in a list with a **negative index**: an index (that must be a negative number) you can use to look up items in an iterable from right to left, instead of left to right. You can use the negative index -1 to look up the last item in an iterable:

```
1  # http://tinyurl.com/hyju2t5
2
3
4  author = "Kafka"
5  author[-1]
```

```
>> a
```

The negative index −2 looks up the second to last item, the negative index −3 looks up the item third to last, and so on:

```
1  # http://tinyurl.com/jtpx7sr
2
3
4  author = "Kafka"
5  author[-2]
6  author[-3]

>> k
>> f
```

Strings are Immutable

Strings, like tuples, are immutable. You cannot change the characters in a string. If you want to change the characters in a string, you have to create a new string:

```
1  # http://tinyurl.com/hsr83lv
2
3
4  ff = "F. Fitzgerald"
5  ff = "F. Scott Fitzgerald"
6  ff

>> 'F. Scott Fitzgerald'
```

Python has several methods for creating new strings from existing strings, which you will learn to use in this chapter.

Concatenation

You can add two (or more) strings together using the addition operator. The result is a string made up of the characters from the first string, followed by the characters from the next string(s). Adding strings together is called concatenation:

```
1  # http://tinyurl.com/h4z5mlg
2
3
4  "cat" + "in" + "hat"

>> 'catinhat'
```

```
1  # http://tinyurl.com/gsrajle
2
3
4  "cat " + " in" + " the" + " hat"
```

>> 'cat in the hat'

String Multiplication

You can multiply a string by a number with the multiplication operator:

```
1  # http://tinyurl.com/zvm9gng
2
3
4  "Sawyer" * 3
```

>> SawyerSawyerSawyer

Change Case

You can change every character in a string to uppercase by calling the upper method on it:

```
1  # http://tinyurl.com/hhancz6
2
3
4  "We hold these truths...".upper()
```

>> 'WE HOLD THESE TRUTHS...'

Similarly, you can change every letter in a string to lowercase by calling the lower method on it:

```
1  # http://tinyurl.com/zkz48u5
2
3
4  "SO IT GOES.".lower()
```

>> 'so it goes.'

You can capitalize the first letter of a sentence by calling the `capitalize` method on a string:

```
1  # http://tinyurl.com/jp5hexn
2
3
4  "four score and...".capitalize()

>> 'Four score and...'
```

Format

You can create a new string using the `format` method, which looks for occurrences of curly brackets { } in the string, and replaces them with the parameters you pass in:

```
1  # http://tinyurl.com/juvguy8
2
3
4  "William {}".format("Faulkner")

>> 'William Faulkner'
```

You can also pass in a variable as a parameter:

```
1  # http://tinyurl.com/zcpt9se
2
3
4  last = "Faulkner"
5  "William {}".format(last)

>> 'William Faulkner'
```

You are not limited to using curly brackets once you can use them in your string as often as you'd like:

```
1  # http://tinyurl.com/z6t6d8n
2
3
4  author = "William Faulkner"
5  year_born = "1897"
6
7
8  "{} was born in {}.".format(author, year_born)
```

>> 'William Faulkner was born in 1897.'

The `format` method is useful if you are creating a string from user input:

```
1   # http://tinyurl.com/gnrdsj9
2
3
4   n1 = input("Enter a noun:")
5   v = input("Enter a verb:")
6   adj = input("Enter an adj:")
7   n2 = input("Enter a noun:")
8
9
10  r = """The {} {} the {} {}
11        """.format(n1,
12                    v,
13                    adj,
14                    n2)
15  print(r)
```

>> Enter a noun:

Your program asks the user to enter two nouns, a verb, and an adjective, then uses the `format` method to create a new string with the input and prints it.

Split

Strings have a method called `split`, which you can use to separate one string into two or more strings. You pass the `split` method a string as a parameter, and it uses that string to divide the original string into multiple strings. For example, you can separate the string `"I jumped over the puddle. It was 12 feet!"` into two different strings by passing the `split` method a period as a parameter:

```
1  # http://tinyurl.com/he8u28o
2
3
4  "Hello.Yes!".split(".")

>> ['Hello', ' Yes!']
```

The result is a list with two items in it: a string made up of all the characters before the period, and a string made up of all the characters after the period.

Join

The `join` method lets you add new characters between every character in a string:

```
1  # http://tinyurl.com/h2pjkso
2
3
4  first_three = "abc"
5  result = "+".join(first_three)
6  result

>> 'a+b+c'
```

You can turn a list of strings into a single string by calling the `join` method on an empty string, and passing in the list as a parameter:

```
1  # http://tinyurl.com/z49e3up
2
3
4  words = ["The",
5          "fox",
6          "jumped",
7          "over",
8          "the",
9          "fence",
10         "."]
11  one = "".join(words)
12  one

>> Thefoxjumpedoverthefence.
```

You can create a string with each word separated by a space by calling the `join` method on a string with a space in it:

```
1   # http://tinyurl.com/h4qq5oy
2
3
4   words = ["The",
5           "fox",
6           "jumped",
7           "over",
8           "the",
9           "fence",
10          "."]
11  one = " ".join(words)
12  one
```

>> The fox jumped over the fence .

Strip Space

You can use the `strip` method to remove leading and trailing whitespace from a string:

```
1   # http://tinyurl.com/jfndhgx
2
3
4   s = "     The           "
5   s = s.strip()
6   s
```

>> 'The'

Replace

The `replace` method replaces every occurrence of a string with another string. The first parameter is the string to replace, and the second parameter is the string to replace the occurrences with:

```
1  # http://tinyurl.com/zha4uwo
2
3
4  equ = "All animals are equal."
5  equ = equ.replace("a", "@")
6  print(equ)
```

>> All @nim@ls @re equ@l.

Find an Index

You can get the index of the first occurrence of a character in a string with the `index` method. Pass in the character you are looking for as a parameter, and the `index` method returns the index of the first occurrence of that character in the string:

```
1  # http://tinyurl.com/hzc6asc
2
3
4  "animals".index("m")
```

>> 3

Python raises an exception if the `index` method does not find a match:

```
1  # http://tinyurl.com/jmtc984
2
3
4  "animals".index("z")
```

>> ValueError: substring not found

If you are not sure if you will find a match, you can use exception handling:

```
1  # http://tinyurl.com/zl6q4fd
2
3
4  try:
5      "animals".index("z")
6  except:
7      print("Not found.")
```

```
>> Not found.
```

In

The in keyword checks if a string is in another string, and returns either True or False:

```
1  # http://tinyurl.com/hsnygwz
2
3
4  "Cat" in "Cat in the hat."
```

```
>> True
```

```
1  # http://tinyurl.com/z9b3e97
2
3
4  "Bat" in "Cat in the hat."
```

```
>> False
```

Put the keyword not in front of the in to check if one string is not in another string:

```
1  # http://tinyurl.com/jz8sygd
2
3  "Potter" not in "Harry"
```

```
>> True
```

Escaping Strings

If you use quotes inside a string, you will get a syntax error:

```
1  # http://tinyurl.com/zj6hc4r
2
3
4  # this code does not work.
5
6
7  "She said "Surely.""
```

```
>> SyntaxError: invalid syntax
```

You can fix this error by prefacing the quotes with backslashes:

```
1  # http://tinyurl.com/jdsrr7e
2
3
4  "She said \"Surely.\""
```

```
>> 'She said "Surely."'
```

```
1  # http://tinyurl.com/zr7o7d7
2
3
4  'She said \"Surely.\"'
```

```
>> 'She said "Surely."'
```

Escaping a string means putting a symbol in front of a character that normally has a special meaning in Python (in this case, a quote), that lets Python know that, in this instance, the quote is meant to represent a character, and not the special meaning. Python uses a backslash for escaping.

You do not need to escape single quotes inside of a string with double quotes:

```
1  # http://tinyurl.com/hoef63o
2
3
4  "She said 'Surely.'"
```

```
>> "She said 'Surely.'"
```

You can also put double quotes inside of single quotes, which is simpler than escaping the double quotes:

```
1  # http://tinyurl.com/zkgfawo
2
3
4  'She said "Surely."'
```

```
>> 'She said "Surely."'
```

Newline

Putting \n inside a string represents a newline:

```
1   # http://tinyurl.com/zyrhaeg
2
3
4   print("line1\nline2\nline3")
```

```
>> line1
>> line2
>> line3
```

Slicing

Slicing is a way to return a new iterable from a subset of the items in another iterable. The syntax for slicing is [iterable][[start_index:end_index]]. The **start index** is the index to start slicing from, and the **end index** is the index to stop slicing at.

Here is how to slice a list:

```
1   # http://tinyurl.com/h2rqj2a
2
3
4   fict = ["Tolstoy",
5           "Camus",
6           "Orwell",
7           "Huxley",
8           "Austin"]
9   fict[0:3]
```

```
>> ['Tolstoy', 'Camus', 'Orwell']
```

With slicing, the start index includes the item at that index, but the end index only includes the item before the end index. Because of this, if you want to slice from "Tolstoy" (index 0) to "Orwell" (index 2), you need to slice from index 0 to index 3.

Here is an example of slicing a string:

```
1  # http://tinyurl.com/hug9euj
2
3
4  ivan = "In place of death there was light."
5
6
7  ivan[0:17]
8  ivan[17:33]

>> 'In place of death'
>> ' there was light.'
```

If your start index is 0, you can leave the start index empty:

```
1  # http://tinyurl.com/judcpx4
2
3
4  ivan = "In place of death there was light."
5
6
7  ivan[:17]

>> 'In place of death'
```

If your end index is the index of the last item in the iterable, you can leave the end index empty:

```
1  # http://tinyurl.com/zqoscn4
2
3
4  ivan = "In place of death there was light."
5
6
7  ivan[17:]

>> ' there was light.'
```

Leaving both the start and end index empty returns the original iterable:

```
1  # http://tinyurl.com/zqvuqoc
2
3
4  ivan = """In place of death there was light."""
5
6
7  ivan[:]
```

>> "In place of death there was light."

Vocabulary

Negative index: An index (that must be a negative number) you can use to look up items in an iterable from right to left, instead of left to right.

Escaping: Putting a symbol in front of a character that normally has a special meaning in Python, which lets Python know that, in this instance, the character is meant to represent a character, and not the special meaning.

Slicing: A way to return a new iterable from a subset of the items in another iterable.

Start index: The index to start slicing from.

End index: The index to stop slicing at.

Challenges

1. Print every character in the string "Camus".

2. Write a program that collects two strings from a user, inserts them into the string "Yesterday I wrote a [response_one]. I sent it to [response_two]!" and prints a new string.

3. Use a method to make the string "aldous Huxley was born in 1894." grammatically correct by capitalizing the first letter in the sentence.

4. Take the string "Where now? Who now? When now?" and call a method that returns a list that looks like: ["Where now?", "Who now?", "When now?"].

5. Take the list ["The", "fox", "jumped", "over", "the", "fence", "."] and turn it into a grammatically correct string. There should be a space between each word, but no space between the word fence and the period that follows it. (Don't forget, you learned a method that turns a list of strings into a single string.)

6. Replace every instance of "s" in "A screaming comes across the sky." with a dollar sign.

7. Use a method to find the first index of the character "m" in the string "Hemingway".

8. Find dialogue in your favorite book (containing quotes) and turn it into a string.

9. Create the string `"three three three"` using concatenation, and then again using multiplication.

10. Slice the string `"It was a bright cold day in April, and the clocks were striking thirteen."` to only include the characters before the comma.

Solutions: http://tinyurl.com/hapm4dx.

Chapter 7. Loops

"Eighty percent of success is showing up."
— Woody Allen

The second program I introduced in this book printed `Hello, World!` a hundred times. It accomplished this using a **loop**: a piece of code that continually executes instructions until a condition defined in the code is satisfied. In this chapter, you will learn about loops and how to use them.

For-Loops

In this section, you will learn how to use a **for-loop**: a loop used to iterate through an iterable. This process is called **iterating**. You can use a `for-loop` to define instructions that execute once for every item in an iterable, and you can access and manipulate each item in the iterable from within the instructions you defined. For example, you could use a `for-loop` to iterate through a list of strings, and use the `upper` method to print each string with all of its characters capitalized.

You can define a `for-loop` using the syntax `for [variable_name] in [iterable_name]: [instructions]` where `[variable_name]` is a variable name of your choosing assigned to the value of each item in the iterable, and `[instructions]` is the code to be executed each time through the loop. Here is an example using a `for-loop` to iterate through the characters of a string:

```
1  # http://tinyurl.com/jya6kpm
2
3
4  name = "Ted"
5  for character in name:
6      print(character)
```

```
>> T
>> e
>> d
```

Each time around the loop, the variable `character` gets assigned to an item in the iterable `name`. The first time around the loop, `T` prints because the variable `character` is assigned the value of the first item in the iterable `name`. The second time around the loop, `e` prints because the variable `character` is assigned the value of the second item in the iterable name. This process continues until every item in the iterable has been assigned to the variable `character`.

Here is an example using a `for-loop` to iterate through the items in a list:

```
1  # http://tinyurl.com/zeftpq8
2
3
4  shows = ["GOT",
5           "Narcos",
6           "Vice"]
7  for show in shows:
8      print(show)
```

```
>> GOT
>> Narcos
>> Vice
```

An example using a `for-loop` to iterate through the items in a tuple:

```
1  # http://tinyurl.com/gpr5a6e
2
3
4  coms = ("A. Development",
5          "Friends",
6          "Always Sunny")
7  for show in coms:
8      print(show)
```

```
>> A. Development
>> Friends
>> Always Sunny
```

And an example using a `for-loop` to iterate through the keys in a dictionary:

```
1   # http://tinyurl.com/jk7do9b
2
3
4   people = {"G. Bluth II":
5                "A. Development",
6                "Barney":
7                "HIMYM",
8                "Dennis":
9                "Always Sunny"
10               }
11
12
13  for character in people:
14      print(character)
```

```
>> Dennis
>> Barney
>> G. Bluth II
```

You can use for-loops to change the items in a mutable iterable, like a list:

```
1   # http://tinyurl.com/j8wvp8c
2
3
4   tv = ["GOT",
5           "Narcos",
6           "Vice"]
7   i = 0
8   for show in tv:
9       new = tv[i]
10      new = new.upper()
11      tv[i] = new
12      i += 1
13
14
15  print(tv)
```

```
>> ['GOT, 'NARCOS', 'VICE']
```

In this example, you used a for-loop to iterate through the list tv. You keep track of the current item in the list using an **index variable**: a variable that holds an integer representing an index in an iterable. The index variable i starts at 0, and is incremented each time around the loop. You use the index variable to get the current item from the list, which you then store in the variable new. Next, you call the upper method on new, save the result, and use your index variable to replace the current item in the list with it. Finally, you increment i so you can look up the next item in the list the next time around the loop.

Because accessing each item and its index in an iterable is so common; Python has another syntax you can use for this:

```
1   # http://tinyurl.com/z45g63j
2
3
4   tv = ["GOT", "Narcos",
5           "Vice"]
6   for i, show in enumerate(tv):
7       new = tv[i]
8       new = new.upper()
9       tv[i] = new
10
11
12  print(tv)
```

>> ['GOT', 'NARCOS', 'VICE']

Instead of iterating through tv, you passed tv to enumerate and iterated through the result, which allowed you to add a new variable i that keeps track of the current index.

You can use for-loops to move data between mutable iterables. For example, you can use two for-loops to take all the strings from two different lists, capitalize each character in them, and put them into a new list:

```
1   # http://tinyurl.com/zcvgklh
2
3
4   tv = ["GOT", "Narcos",
5           "Vice"]
6   coms = ["Arrested Development",
7               "friends",
8               "Always Sunny"]
9   all_shows = []
10
11
12  for show in tv:
13      show = show.upper()
14      all_shows.append(show)
15
16
17  for show in coms:
18      show = show.upper()
19      all_shows.append(show)
20
21
22  print(all_shows)
```

>>   ['GOT', 'NARCOS', 'VICE', 'ARRESTED DEVELOPMENT', 'FRIENDS', 'ALWAYS SUNNY']

In this example, there are three lists: tv, coms, and all_shows. In the first loop, you iterate through all the items in the list tv, use the upper method to capitalize each item in it, and use the append method to add each item to the list all_shows. In the second loop, you do the same thing with the coms list. When you print the list all_shows, it contains all of the items from both lists, with every item capitalized.

Range

You can use the built-in range function to create a sequence of integers, and use a for-loop to iterate through them. The range function takes two parameters: a number where the sequence starts and a number where the sequence stops. The sequence of integers returned by the range function includes the first parameter (the number to start at), but not the second parameter (the number to stop at). Here is an example of using the range function to create a sequence of numbers, and iterate through them:

```
1   # http://tinyurl.com/hh5t8rw
2
3
4   for i in range(1, 11):
5       print(i)

>> 1
...
>> 9
>> 10
```

In this example, you used a for-loop to print each number in the iterable returned by the range function. Programmers often name the variable used to iterate through a list of integers i.

While-Loops

In this section, you will learn how to use a **while-loop**: a loop that executes code as long as an expression evaluates to True. The syntax for a while-loop is while [expression]: [code_to_execute], where [expression] represents the expression that determines whether or not the loop will continue and [code_to_execute] represents the code the loop should execute as long as it does:

```
1   # http://tinyurl.com/j2gwlcy
2
3
4   x = 10
5   while x > 0:
6       print('{}'.format(x))
7       x -= 1
8   print("Happy New Year!")

>> 10
>> 9
>> 8
>> 7
>> 6
>> 5
>> 4
>> 3
>> 2
```

```
>> 1
>> Happy New Year!
```

Your `while-loop` executes its code as long as the expression you defined in its header, x > 0, evaluates to True. The first time around the loop x is 10, and the expression x > 0 evaluates to True. Your `while-loop` code prints the value of x, then decrements x by 1. x now equals 9. The next time around the loop x is printed again, and gets decremented to 8. This process continues until x is decremented to 0, at which point x > 0 evaluates to False, and your loop ends. Python then executes the next line of code after your loop, and prints Happy New Year!

If you define a `while-loop` with an expression that always evaluates to True, your loop will run forever. A loop that never ends is called an **infinite loop**. Here is an example of an infinite loop (be prepared to press control-c on your keyboard in the Python shell to stop the infinite loop from running):

```
1   # http://tinyurl.com/hcwvfk8
2
3
4   while True:
5       print("Hello, World!")
```

```
>> Hello, World!
...
```

Because a `while-loop` runs as long as the expression defined in its header evaluates to True—and True always evaluates to True—this loop will run forever.

Break

You can use a **break-statement** a statement with the keyword `break` to terminate a loop. The following loop will run one hundred times:

```
1   # http://tinyurl.com/zrdh88c
2
3
4   for i in range(0, 100):
5       print(i)
```

```
>> 0
>> 1
...
```

If you add a break-statement, the loop only runs once:

```
1  # http://tinyurl.com/zhxf3uk
2
3
4  for i in range(0, 100):
5      print
6      break
```

>> 0

As soon as Python hits the break-statement, the loop ends. You can use a while-loop and the break keyword to write a program that keeps asking the user for input until they type q to quit:

```
1   # http://tinyurl.com/jmak8tr
2
3
4   qs = ["What is your name?",
5         "What is your fav. color?",
6         "What is your quest?"]
7   n = 0
8   while True:
9       print("Type q to quit")
10      a = input(qs[n])
11      if a == "q":
12          break
13      n = (n + 1) % 3
```

>> Type q to quit
>> What is your name?

Each time through the loop, your program asks the user one of the questions in your qs list.

n is an index variable. Each time around the loop, you assign n to the evaluation of the expression (n + 1) % 3, which enables you to cycle indefinitely through every question in your qs list. The first time around the loop, n starts at 0. Next, n is assigned the value of the expression (0 + 1) % 3, which evaluates to 1. Then, n is assigned to the value of (1 + 1) % 3, which evaluates to 2, because whenever the first number in an expression using modulo is smaller than the second, the answer is the first number. Finally, n is assigned the value of (2 + 1) % 3, which evaluates back to 0.

Continue

You can use a **continue-statement**—a statement with the keyword continue — to stop the current iteration of a loop and move on to the next iteration of it. Say you want to print all the numbers from 1 to 5, except the number 3. You can achieve this using a for-loop and a continue-statement:

```
1  # http://tinyurl.com/hflun4p
2
3
4  for i in range(1, 6):
5      if i == 3:
6          continue
7      print(i)
```

```
>> 1
>> 2
>> 4
>> 5
```

In this loop, when i equals 3, your continue-statement executes, and instead of causing your loop to exit completely—like the break keyword would—the loop persists. The loop moves on to the next iteration, skipping any code that would have executed. When i equals 3, and Python executes the continue-statement, Python does not print the number 3.

You can achieve the same result using a while-loop and a continue-statement:

```
1   # http://tinyurl.com/gp7forl
2
3
4   i = 1
5   while i <= 5:
6       if i == 3:
7           i += 1
8           continue
9       print(i)
10      i += 1
```

>> 1
>> 2
>> 4
>> 5

Nested Loops

You can combine loops in various ways. For example, you can have one loop inside of a loop or a loop inside a loop inside a loop. There is no limit to the number of loops you can have inside of other loops, although you want to limit this. When a loop is inside another loop, the second loop is nested in the first loop. In this situation, the loop with another loop inside it is called an **outer loop**, and the nested loop is called an **inner loop**. When you have a nested loop, the inner loop iterates through its iterable once for each time around the outer loop:

```
1   # http://tinyurl.com/gqjxjtq
2
3
4   for i in range(1, 3):
5       print(i)
6       for letter in ["a", "b", "c"]:
7           print(letter)
```

>> 1
>> a
>> b
>> c
>> 2
>> a
>> b
>> c

The nested `for-loop` will iterate through the list `["a", "b", "c"]` however many times the outer loop runs—in this case, twice. If you changed your outer loop to run three times, the inner loop would iterate through its list three times as well.

You can use two `for-loops` to add each number in a list to all the numbers in another list:

```
1   # http://tinyurl.com/z7duawp
2
3
4   list1 = [1, 2, 3, 4]
5   list2 = [5, 6, 7, 8]
6   added = []
7   for i in list1:
8       for j in list2:
9           added.append(i + j)
10
11
12  print(added)
```

>> [6, 7, 8, 9, 7, 8, 9, 10, 8, 9, 10, 11, 9, 10, 11, 12]

The first loop iterates through every integer in `list1`. For each item in it, the second loop iterates through each integer in its own iterable, adds it to the integer from `list1` and appends the result to the list `added`. I named the variable `j` in the second `for-loop`, because I already used the variable name `i` in the first loop.

You can nest a `for-loop` inside a `while-loop`, and vice versa:

```
1   # http://tinyurl.com/hnprmmv
2
3
4   while input('y or n?') != 'n':
5       for i in range(1, 6):
6           print(i)
```

>> y or n?y
1
2
3

```
4
5
y or n?y
1
2
3
4
5
y or n?n
>>>
```

This program will print the numbers 1-5 until the user enters n.

Vocabulary

Loop: A piece of code that continually executes instructions until a condition defined in the code is satisfied.

Iterating: Using a loop to access each item in an iterable.

For-loop: A loop used to iterate through an iterable, like a string, list, tuple, or dictionary.

Index variable: A variable that holds an integer representing an index in an iterable.

While-loop: A loop that executes code as long as an expression evaluates to True.

Infinite loop: A loop that never ends.

Break-statement: A statement with the keyword break in it used to terminate a loop.

Continue-statement: A statement with the keyword continue used to stop the current iteration of a loop and move on to the next iteration of it.

Outer loop: A loop with a nested loop inside it.

Inner loop: A loop nested in another loop.

Challenges

1. Print each item in the following list: ["The Walking Dead", "Entourage", "The Sopranos", "The Vampire Diaries"].
2. Print all the numbers from 25 to 50.
3. Print each item in the list from the first challenge and their indexes.
4. Write a program with an infinite loop (with the option to type q to quit) and a list of numbers. Each time through the loop ask the user to guess a number on the list and tell them whether or not they guessed correctly.
5. Multiply all the numbers in the list [8, 19, 148, 4] with all the numbers in the list [9, 1, 33, 83], and append each result to a third list.

Solutions: http://tinyurl.com/z2m2ll5.

Chapter 8. Modules

"Perseverance and spirit have done wonders in all ages."
—George Washington

Imagine you wrote a program with 10,000 lines of code. If you put all of the code in one file, it would be difficult to navigate. Every time there was an error or exception, you would have to scroll through 10,000 lines of code to find the one line causing the problem. Programmers solve this issue by dividing large programs into multiple pieces, called **modules** another name for a Python file with code in it containing each piece. Python allows you to use code from one module in another module. Python also has **built-in modules**, modules that are built into Python and contain important functionality. In this chapter, you learn about modules and how to use them.

Importing Built-In Modules

To use a module, you must first **import** it: which means writing code, so Python knows where to look for it. You can import a module with the syntax import [module_name]. Replace [module_name] with the name of the module you are importing. Once you've imported a module, you can use variables and functions from it.

Python has many different modules, including a math module containing math-related functionality. You can find a list of all of Python's built-in modules at https://docs.python.org/3/py-modindex.html. Here is how to import Python's math module:

```
1  # http://tinyurl.com/h3ds93u
2
3
4  import math
```

Once you've imported a module, you can use code from it with the syntax [module_name].[code], replacing [module_name] with the name of a module you already imported, and [code] with the name of the function or variable you want to use from it. The following is an example of importing and using the pow function from the math module, which takes two parameters, x and y, and raises x by y:

```
1   # http://tinyurl.com/hyjo59s
2
3
4   import math
5
6
7   math.pow(2, 3)
```

>> 8.0

First, import the math module at the top of your file. You should import all of your modules at the top of your file to make it easy to see which ones you are using in your program. Next, call the pow function with math.pow(2, 3). The function returns 8.0 as the result.

The random module is another built-in module. You can use a function from it called randint to generate a random integer: you pass it two integers, and it returns a random integer between them:

```
 1   # http://tinyurl.com/hr3fppn
 2
 3
 4   # The output might not be 52
 5   # when you run it—it's random!
 6
 7
 8   import random
 9
10
11   random.randint(0,100)
```

>> 52

You can use the built-in statistics module to calculate the mean, median, and mode in an iterable of numbers:

```
 1  # http://tinyurl.com/jrnznoy
 2
 3
 4  import statistics
 5
 6  # mean
 7  nums = [1, 5, 33, 12, 46, 33, 2]
 8  statistics.mean(nums)
 9
10
11  # median
12  statistics.median(nums)
13
14
15  # mode
16  statistics.mode(nums)
```

```
>> 18.857142857142858
>> 12
>> 33
```

Use the built-in `keyword` module to check if a string is a Python keyword:

```
 1  # http://tinyurl.com/zjphfho
 2
 3
 4  import keyword
 5
 6
 7  keyword.iskeyword("for")
 8  keyword.iskeyword("football")
```

```
>> True
>> False
```

Importing Other Modules

In this section, you are going to create a module, import it in another module, and use the code from it. First, create a new folder on your computer called `tstp`. Inside that folder, create a file called `hello.py`. Add the following code to `hello.py` and save the file:

```
1   # http://tinyurl.com/z5v9hk3
2
3
4   def print_hello():
5       print("Hello")
```

Inside your tstp folder, create another Python file called project.py. Add the following code to project.py, and save the file:

```
1   # http://tinyurl.com/j4xv728
2
3
4   import hello
5
6
7   hello.print_hello()
```

>> Hello

In this example, you used the import keyword to use code from your first module in your second module.

When you import a module, all of the code in it executes. Create a module named module1.py with the following code:

```
1   # http://tinyurl.com/zgyddhp
2
3
4   # code in module1
5   print("Hello!")
```

>> Hello!

The code from module1.py will run when you import it in another module named module2.py:

```
1   # http://tinyurl.com/jamt9dy
2
3
4   # code in module2
5   import hello
```

```
>> Hello!
```

This behavior can be inconvenient. For instance, you might have test code in your module that you do not want to run when you import it. You can solve this problem by putting all of the code in your module within the statement if __name__ == "__main__". For example, you could change the code in module1.py from the previous example to the following:

```
1  # http://tinyurl.com/j2xdzc7
2
3
4  # code in module1
5  if __name__ == "__main__":
6      print("Hello!")
```

```
>> Hello!
```

When you run this program, the output is still the same. But when you import it from module2.py, the code from module1.p no longer runs, and Hello! does not print:

```
1  # http://tinyurl.com/jjccxds
2
3
4  # code in module2
5  import hello
```

Vocabulary

Module: Another name for a Python file with code in it.
Built-in module: Modules that come with Python that contain important functionality.
Import: Writing code that lets Python know where to look for a module you plan on using.

Challenges

1. Call a different function from the statistics module.
2. Create a module named cubed with a function that takes a number as a parameter, and returns the number cubed. Import and call the function from another module.

Solutions: http://tinyurl.com/hlnsdot.

Chapter 9. Files

"Self-education is, I firmly believe, the only kind of education there is."
—Isaac Asimov

You can use Python to work with files. For example, you can use Python to read data from a file and to write data to a file. **Reading** data from a file means accessing the file's data. **Writing** data to a file means adding or changing data in the file. In this chapter, you will learn the basics of working with files.

Writing to Files

The first step to working with a file is to open it with Python's built-in `open` function. The `open` function takes two parameters: a string representing the path to the file to open and a string representing the mode to open the file in.

The path to a file, or **file path**, represents the location on your computer where a file resides. For example, `/Users/bob/st.txt` is the file path to a file called `st.txt`. Each word separated by a slash is the name of a folder. Together, it represents the location of a file. If a file path only has the name of the file (with no folders separated by slashes), Python will look for it in whatever folder you are running your program from. You should not write a file path yourself. Unix-like operating systems and Windows use a different type of slash in their file paths. To avoid problems with your program working across different operating systems, you should always create file paths using Python's builtin `os module`. The `path` function in it takes each folder in a file path as a parameter and builds the file path for you:

```
1  # http://tinyurl.com/hkqfkar
2
3
4  import os
5  os.path.join("Users",
6               "bob",
7               "st.txt")
```

```
>> 'Users/bob/st.txt'
```

Creating file paths with the `path` function ensures they will work on any operating system. Working with file paths can still be tricky. Visit https://theselftaughtprogrammer.io/filepaths if you are having trouble.

The mode you pass to the open function determines the actions you will be able to perform on the file you open. Here are a few of the modes you can open a file in:

"r" opens a file for reading only.

"w" opens a file for writing only. Overwrites the file if the file exists. If the file does not exist, creates a new file for writing.

"w+" opens a file for reading and writing. Overwrites the existing file if the file exists. If the file does not exist, creates a new file for reading and writing.[5]

The open function returns an object, called a **file object**, which you can use to read and/or write to your file. When you use the mode "w", the open function creates a new file, if it doesn't already exist, in the directory your program is running in.

You can then use the write method on the file object to write to the file, and the close method to close it. If you open a file using the open method, you must close it with the close method. If you use the open method on multiple files and forget to close them, it can cause problems in your program. Here is an example of opening a file, writing to it, and closing it:

```
1  # http://tinyurl.com/zfgczj5
2
3
4  st = open("st.txt", "w")
5  st.write("Hi from Python!")
6  st.close()
```

In this example, you use the open function to open the file and save the file object it returns in the variable st. Then you call the write method on st, which accepts a string as a parameter and writes it to the new file Python created. Finally, you close your file by calling the close method on the file object.

Automatically Closing Files

There is a second preferred syntax to open files that prevents you from having to remember to close them. To use this syntax, you put all of your code that needs access to the file object inside a **with-statement**: a compound statement with an action that automatically occurs when Python leaves it.

The syntax for opening a file using a `with-statement` is with `open([file_path],[mode])` as `[variable_name]`: `[your_code]`. `[file_path]` represents the filepath, `[mode]` represents the mode to open the file in, `[variable_name]` represents the name of the variable the file object is assigned to, and `[your_code]` represents the code that has access to the variable the file object is assigned to.

When you use this syntax to open a file, it automatically closes after the last suite in `[your_code]` executes. Here is the example from the previous section using this new syntax to open, write to, and close a file:

```
1  # http://tinyurl.com/jt9guu2
2
3
4  with open("st.txt", "w") as f:
5      f.write("Hi from Python!")
```

As long as you are inside the `with-statement`, you can access the file object—in this case, you named it `f`. As soon as Python finishes running all the code in the `with-statement`, Python closes the file for you.

Reading from Files

If you want to read the file, you pass in `"r"` as the second parameter to `open`. Then you call the `read` method on your file object, which returns an iterable containing each line of the file:

```
1   # http://tinyurl.com/hmuamr7
2
3
4   # make sure you've
5   # created the file from
6   # the previous example
7
8
9   with open("st.txt", "r") as f:
10      print(f.read())
```

`>> Hi from Python!`

You can only call `read` on a file once, without closing and reopening it to get its contents, so you should save the file contents in a variable or container if you need to use them later in your program. Here is how to save the contents from the file in the previous example in a list:

```
1   # http://tinyurl.com/hkzhxdz
2
3
4   my_list = list()
5
6
7   with open("st.txt", "r") as f:
8       my_list.append(f.read())
9
10
11  print(my_list)
```

```
>> ['Hi from Python!']
```

Now you can access this data later in your program.

CSV Files

Python comes with a built-in module that allows you to work with **CSV files**. A CSV file has a `.csv` extension that separates data using commas (CSV stands for Comma Separated Values). Programs that manage spreadsheets like Excel often use CSV files. Each piece of data separated by a comma in a CSV file represents a cell in a spreadsheet, and every line represents a row. A **delimiter** is a symbol, like a comma or a vertical bar |, used to separate data in a CSV file. Here are the contents of a CSV file named `self_taught.csv`:

one,two,three four,five,six

You could load this file into Excel, and one, two, and three would each get cells in the first row of the spreadsheet, and four, five, and six would each get cells in the second row.

You can use a `with-statement` to open a CSV file, but inside the `with-statement` you need to use the `csv` module to convert the file object into a `csv` object. The `csv` module has a method called `writer` that accepts a file object and a delimiter. The `writer` method returns a `csv` object that has a method called `writerow`. The `writerow` method accepts a list as a parameter, and you can use it to write to a CSV file. Every item in the list gets written — separated by the delimiter you pass to the `writer` method — to a row in the

CSV file. The `writerow` method only creates one row, so you have to call it twice to create two rows:

```
1   # http://tinyurl.com/go9wepf
2
3
4   import csv
5
6
7   with open("st.csv", "w", newline='') as f:
8       w = csv.writer(f,
9                        delimiter=",")
10      w.writerow(["one",
11                   "two",
12                   "three"])
13      w.writerow(["four",
14                   "five",
15                   "six"])
```

This program creates a new file called `st.csv`, and when you open it in a text editor, it looks like this:

one,two,three
four,five,six

If you load the file into Excel (or Google Sheets, a free Excel alternative) the commas disappear; but one, two, and three are cells in row one; and four, five, and six are cells in row two.

You can also use the `csv` module to read the contents of a file. To read from a CSV file you first pass in `"r"` as the second parameter to the `open` function to open the file for reading. Then, inside the `with-statement`, you call the reader method, passing in the file object and a comma as the delimiter, which returns an iterable you can use to access each row in the file.

```
 1 │ # http://tinyurl.com/gvcdgxf
 2 │
 3 │
 4 │ # make sure you've created
 5 │ # the file from the previous
 6 │ # example
 7 │
 8 │
 9 │ import csv
10 │
11 │
12 │ with open("st.csv", "r") as f:
13 │     r = csv.reader(f, delimiter=",")
14 │     for row in r:
15 │         print(",".join(row))
```

>> one,two,three
>> four,five,six

In this example, you open st.csv for reading and convert it to a csv object using the reader method. You then iterate through the csv object using a loop. Each time around the loop, you call the join method on a comma to add a comma between each piece of data in the file and print the contents the way they appear in the original file (separated by commas).

Vocabulary

Reading: Accessing the file's content.
Writing: Adding or changing data in the file.
File path: The location on your computer where a file resides.
With-statement: A compound statement with an action that automatically occurs when Python leaves it.
File object: An object you can use to read or write to a file.
CSV file: A file with a .csv extension that separates data using commas (CSV stands for Comma Separated Values). Frequently used in programs that manage spreadsheets, like Excel.
Delimiter: A symbol, like a comma, used to separate data in a CSV file.

Challenges

1. Find a file on your computer and print its contents using Python.

2. Write a program that asks a user a question, and saves their answer to a file.

3. Take the items in this list of lists: [["Top Gun", "Risky Business", "Minority Report"], ["Titanic", "The Revenant", "Inception"], ["Training Day", "Man on Fire", "Flight"]] and write them to a CSV file. The data from each list should be a row in the file, with each item in the list separated by a comma.

Solutions: http://tinyurl.com/hll6t3q.

Chapter 10. Bringing It All Together

"All I have learned, I learned from books."
—Abraham Lincoln

In this chapter, you are going to combine the concepts you've learned so far and build a text-based game, the classic Hangman. If you've never played Hangman, here's how it works:

1. Player One picks a secret word and draws a line for each letter in it (you will use an underscore to represent each line).
2. Player Two tries to guess the word one letter at a time.
3. If Player Two guesses a letter correctly, Player One replaces the corresponding underscore with the correct letter. In this version of the game, if a letter appears twice in a word, you have to guess it twice.
OR
If Player Two guesses incorrectly, Player One draws a body part of a hanged stick figure (starting with the head).
4. If Player Two completes the word before the drawing of the hangman is complete, they win. If not, they lose.

In your program, the computer will be Player One, and the person guessing will be Player Two. Are you ready to build Hangman?

Hangman

Here is the beginning of your Hangman code:

```
1   # http://tinyurl.com/jhrvs94
2
3
4   def hangman(word):
5       wrong = 0
6       stages = ["",
7                 "
                   _____         ",
8                 "|                 ",
9                 "|          |      ",
10                "|          0      ",
11                "|         /|\     ",
12                "|         / \     ",
13                "|                 "
14                ]
15      rletters = list(word)
16      board = ["__"] * len(word)
17      win = False
18      print("Welcome to Hangman")
```

First, you create a function called hangman to store the game. The function accepts a variable called word as a parameter; this is the word Player Two has to guess. You use another variable, wrong, to keep track of how many incorrect letters Player Two has guessed.

The variable stages is a list filled with strings you will use to draw your hangman. When Python prints each string in the stages list on a new line, a picture of a hangman forms. The variable rletters is a list containing each character in the variable word that keeps track of which letters are left to guess.

The variable board is a list of strings used to keep track of the hints you display to Player Two, e.g., c__t if the word is cat (and Player Two has already correctly guessed c and t). You use ["__"] * len(word) to populate the board list, with two underscores for every character in the variable word. For example, if the word is cat, board starts as ["__", "__", "__"].

You also have a `win` variable that starts as `False`, to keep track of whether Player Two has won the game yet. Next, you print `Welcome to Hangman`.

The next part of your code is a loop that keeps the game going:

```
1   # http://tinyurl.com/ztrp5jc
2   while wrong < len(stages) - 1:
3       print("\n")
4       msg = "Guess a letter"
5       char = input(msg)
6       if char in rletters:
7           cind = rletters.index(char)
8           board[cind] = char
9           rletters[cind] = '$'
10      else:
11          wrong += 1
12      print((" ".join(board)))
13      e = wrong + 1
14      print("\n".join(stages[0: e]))
15      if "__" not in board:
16          print("You win!")
17          print(" ".join(board))
18          win = True
19          break
```

Your loop (and game) continues as long as the variable `wrong` is less than the `len(stages)` - 1. The variable `wrong` keeps track of the number of wrong letters Player Two has guessed, so as soon as Player Two guesses more wrong letters than the number of strings that make up the hangman (the number of strings in the `stages` list), the game is over. You have to subtract 1 from the length of the `stages` list to compensate for the fact that the `stages` list starts counting from 0, and `wrong` starts counting at 1.

Once you are inside your loop, print a blank space to make the game look nice when it prints in the shell. Then, collect Player Two's guess with the built-in `input` function and store the value in the variable `guess`.

If `guess` is in `rletters` (the list that keeps track of the letters in the word that Player Two hasn't guessed yet), the player guessed correctly. If the player guessed correctly, you need to update your `board` list, which you use later in the game to display the letters remaining. If Player Two guessed c, you would change your `board` list to `["c", "__", "__"]`.

To do this, you use the index method on your rletters list to get the first index of the letter Player Two guessed, and use it to replace the underscore in board at the index with the correctly guessed letter.

There is one problem with this. Because index only returns the first index of the character you are looking for, your code will not work if the variable word has more than one of the same character. To get around this, modify rletters by replacing the character that was correctly guessed with a dollar sign, so the next time around the loop, the index function will find the next occurrence of the letter (if there is one) and it won't stop at the first occurrence.

If on the other hand, if the player guesses an incorrect letter, you increment wrong by 1.

Next, you print the scoreboard and your hangman using the board and stages lists. The code that prints the scoreboard is ' '.join(board).

Printing the hangman is trickier. When each of the strings in your stages list prints on a new line, a complete picture of a hangman prints. You can create the entire hangman by printing '\n'.join(stages), which adds a new line to each string in the stages list so that each string in the list prints on a separate line.

To print your hangman at whatever stage the game is at, you slice your stages list. You start at stage 0, and slice up to the stage you are at (represented by the variable wrong) plus one. You add one because when you are slicing, the end slice does not get included in the result. This slice gives you only the strings you need to print the version of the hangman you are currently at.

Finally, you check if Player Two won the game. If there are no more underscores in the board list, they guessed all the letters and won the game. If Player Two won, you print You win! It was: and the word they correctly guessed. You also set the variable win to True, which breaks you out of your loop.

Once you break out of your loop, if Player Two won, you do nothing—the program is over. If they lost, the variable win is False. If that is the case, you print the full hangman and You lose!, followed by the word they couldn't guess:

```
1  # http://tinyurl.com/zqklqxo
2  if not win:
3      print("\n".join(stages[0: wrong]))
4      print("You lose! It was {}.".format(word))
```

Here is your complete code:

```
1   # http://tinyurl.com/h9q2cpc
2
3
4   def hangman(word):
5       wrong = 0
6       stages = ["",
7                     "_____        ",
8                     "|              ",
9                     "|        |     ",
10                    "|        0     ",
11                    "|       /|\    ",
12                    "|       / \    ",
13                    "|              "
14                    ]
15      rletters = list(word)
16      board = ["__"] * len(word)
17      win = False
18      print("Welcome to Hangman")
19      while wrong < len(stages) - 1:
20          print("\n")
21          msg = "Guess a letter"
22          char = input(msg)
23          if char in rletters:
24              cind = rletters.index(char)
25              board[cind] = char
26              rletters[cind] = '$'
27          else:
28              wrong += 1
29          print((" ".join(board)))
30          e = wrong + 1
31          print("\n".join(stages[0: e]))
32          if "__" not in board:
33              print("You win!")
34              print(" ".join(board))
35              win = True
36              break
37      if not win:
38          print("\n".join(stages[0: wrong]))
39          print("You lose! It was {}.".format(word))
40
41
42  hangman("cat")
```

Challenge

1. Modify the game, so a word is selected randomly from a list of words.

Solution: http://tinyurl.com/j7rb8or.

Chapter 11. Practice

"Practice doesn't make perfect. Practice makes myelin, and myelin makes perfect."
—Daniel Coyle

If this is your first programming book, I recommend spending time practicing before moving on to the next section. The following is some resources to explore and advice on what to do if you are stuck.

Read

1. https://softwareengineering.stackexchange.com/questions/44177/what-is-the-single-most-effective-thing-you-did-to-improve-your-programming-skil

Other Resources

I've compiled a list of programming resources at https://www.theselftaughtprogrammer. io/resources.

Getting Help

If you get stuck, I have a few suggestions. First, post your question in the Self- Taught Programmers Facebook group located at facebook.com/groups/ selftaughtprogrammers. The group is a community of friendly programmers (and aspiring ones) that can help answer any questions you have.

I also recommend checking out stackoverflow.com, a website where you can post programming questions and get answers from members of the community.

I created an online course based on this book (plus bonus content) you might find helpful as well. It is available at udemy.com/course/self-taught-programmer. If you need additional help, I offer a mentorship program at goselftaught.com.

Learning to rely on other people's help was an important lesson for me. Struggling to figure things out is a major part of the learning process; but at some point, it becomes counterproductive. In the past, when I worked on projects, I used to struggle beyond the point of productivity. If that happens today, I post a question online, if I can't find the answer there already. Every time I've posted a question online, someone has answered it. To that end, I can't say enough about how helpful and friendly the programming community is.

Part II
Introduction to Object-Oriented Programming

Chapter 12. Programming Paradigms

"There are only two kinds of languages: the ones people complain about and the ones nobody uses."
—Bjarne Stroustrup

A **programming paradigm** is a style of programming. There are many different programming paradigms. To program professionally, you need to learn either the object-oriented or functional programming paradigms. In this chapter, you will learn about procedural programming, functional programming, and object-oriented programming—with a focus on object-oriented programming

State

One of the fundamental differences between the various programming paradigms is the handling of **state**. State is the value of a program's variables while it is running. **Global state** is the value of a program's global variables while it is running.

Procedural Programming

In Part I, you programmed using the **procedural programming** paradigm: a programming style in which you write a sequence of steps moving toward a solution—with each step changing the program's state. In procedural programming, you write code to "do this, then that":

```
1  # http://tinyurl.com/jv2rrl8
2
3
4  x = 2
5  y = 4
6  z = 8
7  xyz = x + y + z
8  xyz

>> 14
```

Each line of code in this example changes the program's state. First, you define x, then y, then z. Finally, you define the value of xyz.

When you program procedurally, you store data in global variables and manipulate it with functions:

```
 1  # http://tinyurl.com/gldykam
 2
 3
 4  rock = []
 5  country = []
 6
 7
 8  def collect_songs():
 9      song = "Enter a song."
10      ask = "Type r or c. q to quit"
11
12
13      while True:
14          genre = input(ask)
15          if genre == "q":
16              break
17
18
19          if genre == "r":
20              rk = input(song)
21              rock.append(rk)
22
23
24          elif genre =="c":
25              cy = input(song)
26              country.append(cy)
27
28
29          else:
30              print("Invalid.")
31      print(rock)
32      print(country)
33
34
35  collect_songs()
```

>> Type r or c. q to quit:

Procedural programming is fine when building small programs like this, however, because you store all of your program's state in global variables, you run into problems when your program becomes larger. The problem with relying on global variables is that they cause unexpected errors. When your program becomes large, you start using global variables in multiple functions throughout your program, and it becomes impossible to keep track of all the places a global variable is modified. For example, a function might change the value of a global variable, and later in the program, a second function might change the same global variable, because the programmer who wrote the second function forgot the first function already modified it. This situation frequently occurs and corrupts a program's data.

As your program grows in complexity, the number of global variables in it increases. When you combine this increase with the growth in the number of functions your program needs to handle new functionality, which all modify the global variables, your program quickly becomes impossible to maintain. Furthermore, this approach to programming relies on **side effects**. A side effect is changing the state of a global variable. When you program procedurally, you will often run into unintended side effects such as accidentally incrementing a variable twice.

This problem led to the development of the object-oriented and functional programming paradigms, and they both take different approaches to address it.

Functional Programming

Functional programming originates from the lambda calculus: the smallest universal programming language in the world (created by the mathematician Alonzo Church). Functional programming addresses the problems that arise in procedural programming by eliminating global state. A functional programmer relies on functions that do not use or change global state, the only state they use are the parameters you pass to the function. The result a function returns is usually passed on to another function. A functional programmer can thus avoid global state by passing it from function to function. Eliminating global state removes side effects and the problems that come with them.

There is a lot of jargon in functional programming, and Mary Rose Cook cuts through it with her definition, "Functional code is characterized by one thing: the absence of side effects. It doesn't rely on data outside the current function, and it doesn't change data that exists outside the current function."[6] She follows her definition with an example of a function that has side effects:

```
1  # http://tinyurl.com/gu9jpco
2
3
4  a = 0
5
6
7  def increment():
8      global a
9      a += 1
```

And a function with no side effects:

```
1  # http://tinyurl.com/z27k2yl
2
3
4  def increment(a):
5      return a + 1
```

The first function has side effects because it relies on data outside of itself, and changes data outside of the current function—it incremented a global variable. The second function does not have side effects because it does not rely on or change any data outside of itself.

One advantage of functional programming is that it eliminates an entire category of errors caused by global state (there is no global state in functional programming). A disadvantage of functional programming is certain problems are easier to conceptualize with state. For example, it is simpler to conceptualize designing a user interface with global state than a user interface without global state. If you want to write a program with a button that toggles a picture between being shown to the user and being invisible, it is easier to think about how to create such a button by writing a program with global state. You could create a global variable that is either True or False that hides or reveals the picture, depending on its current value. It is harder to conceptualize designing a button like this without global state.

Object-Oriented Programming

The **object-oriented** programming paradigm also addresses the problems that arise in procedural programming by eliminating global state, but instead of storing state in functions, it is stored in objects. In object-oriented programming, **classes** define a set of objects that can interact with each other. Classes are a mechanism for the programmer to classify and group together similar objects. Think of a bag of oranges. Each orange is an object. All oranges have the same attributes, such as color and weight, but the values of these attributes vary from one orange to the next. You can use a class to model oranges and create orange objects with different values. For instance, you can define a class that allows you to create an orange object that is dark orange and weighs 10 oz, and an orange object that is light orange and weighs 12 oz.

Every object is an **instance** of a class. If you define a class called Orange, and create two Orange objects, each one is an instance of the class Orange; they have the same data type—Orange. You can use the terms object and instance interchangeably. When you define a class, all of the instances of that class will be similar: They all have the attributes defined in the class they are an instance of, such as color or weight for a class representing an orange—but each instance can have different values for these attributes.

In Python, a class is a compound statement with a header and suites. You define a class with the syntax class [name]: [suites] where [name] is the name of the class and [suites] are the class' suites you define. By convention, classes in Python always start with a capital letter, and you write them in camelCase—which means if a class name has more than one word, the first letters of all the words should be capitalized LikeThis, instead of separated by an underscore (the convention for function names). A suite in a class can be a simple statement or a compound statement called a **method**. Methods are like functions, but you define them inside of a class, and you can only call them on the object the class creates (like you did in Part I when you called methods like "hello".upper() on strings). Method names, like function names, should be all lowercase with words separated by underscores.

You define methods with the same syntax as functions, with two differences: you must define a method as a suite in a class, and it has to accept at least one parameter (except in special cases). By convention, you always name the first parameter of a method self. You have to define at least one parameter when you create a method, because when you call a method on an object, Python automatically passes the object that called the method to the method as a parameter:

```
1  # http://tinyurl.com/zrmjape
2
3
4  class Orange:
5      def __init__(self):
6          print("Created!")
```

You can use self to define an **instance variable**: a variable that belongs to an object. If you create multiple objects, they can all have different instance variable values. You can define instance variables with the syntax self.[variable_name] = [variable_value]. You normally define instance variables inside of a special method called __init__ (which stands for initialize) that Python calls when you create an object:

Here is an example of a class that represents an orange:

```
1  # http://tinyurl.com/hrf6cus
2
3
4  class Orange:
5      def __init__(self, w, c):
6          self.weight = w
7          self.color = c
8          print("Created!")
```

The code in __init__ executes when you create an Orange object (which does not happen in this example) and creates two instance variables: weight and color. You can use these variables like regular variables, in any method in your class. When you create an Orange object, the code in __init__ also prints Created! Any method surrounded by double underscores, like __init__, is called a **magic method**: a method Python uses for special purposes like creating an object.

You can create a new Orange object with the same syntax you use to call a function — [classname]([parameters]), replacing [classname] with the name of the class you want to use to create the object and replacing [parameters] with the parameters __init__ accepts. You do not have to pass in self; Python passes it in automatically. Creating a new object is called **instantiating a class**:

```
1  # http://tinyurl.com/jlc7pvk
2
3
4  class Orange:
5      def __init__(self, w, c):
6          self.weight = w
7          self.color = c
8          print("Created!")
9
10
11 or1 = Orange(10, "dark orange")
12 print(or1)
```

```
>> Created!
>> <__main__.Orange object at 0x101a787b8>
```

After the class definition, you instantiate the Orange class with the code Orange(10, "dark orange") and Created! prints. Then, you print the Orange object itself, and Python tells you it is an Orange object and gives you its location in memory (the location in memory printed on your computer will not be the same as this example).

Once you've created an object, you can get the value of its instance variables with the syntax [object_name].[variable_name]:

```
1   # http://tinyurl.com/grwzeo4
2
3
4   class Orange:
5       def __init__(self, w, c):
6           self.weight = w
7           self.color = c
8           print("Created!")
9
10
11  or1 = Orange(10, "dark orange")
12  print(or1.weight)
13  print(or1.color)
```

```
>> Created!
>> 10
>> dark orange
```

You can change the value of an instance variable with the syntax [object_name].[variable_name] = [new_value]:

```
1   # http://tinyurl.com/jsxgw44
2
3
4   class Orange:
5       def __init__(self, w, c):
6           self.weight = w
7           self.color = c
8           print("Created!")
9
10
11  or1 = Orange(10, "dark orange")
12  or1.weight = 100
13  or1.color = "light orange"
14
15
16  print(or1.weight)
17  print(or1.color)
```

```
>> Created!
>> 100
>> light orange
```

Although the instance variables color and weight started with the values "dark orange" and 10, you were able to change their values to "light orange" and 100.

You can use the Orange class to create multiple oranges:

```
1   # http://tinyurl.com/jrmxlmo
2
3
4   class Orange:
5       def __init__(self, w, c):
6           self.weight = w
7           self.color = c
8           print("Created!")
9
10
11  or1 = Orange(4, "light orange")
12  or2 = Orange(8, "dark orange")
13  or3 = Orange(14, "yellow")
```

```
>> Created!
>> Created!
>> Created!
```

There is more to an orange than its physical properties, like color and weight. `Oranges` also do things, like rot, that you can model with methods. Here is how you can give an `Orange` object the ability to rot:

```
 1  # http://tinyurl.com/zcp32pz
 2
 3
 4  class Orange():
 5      def __init__(self, w, c):
 6          """weights are in oz"""
 7          self.weight = w
 8          self.color = c
 9          self.mold = 0
10          print("Created!")
11
12
13      def rot(self, days, temp):
14          self.mold = days * temp
15
16
17  orange = Orange(6, "orange")
18  print(orange.mold)
19  orange.rot(10, 98)
20  print(orange.mold)
```

```
>> Created!
>> 0
>> 98.0
```

The method `rot` accepts two parameters: the numbers of days since someone picked the orange, and the average temp during that time. When you call it, the method uses a formula to increment the instance variable `mold`, which works because you can change the value of any instance variable inside of any method. Now, the orange can rot.

You can define multiple methods in a class. Here is an example of modeling a rectangle with a method to calculate its area, and another method to change its size:

```
1   # http://tinyurl.com/j28qoox
2
3
4   class Rectangle():
5       def __init__(self, w, l):
6           self.width = w
7           self.len = l
8
9
10      def area(self):
11          return self.width * self.len
12
13
14      def change_size(self, w, l):
15          self.width = w
16          self.len = l
17
18
19  rectangle = Rectangle(10, 20)
20  print(rectangle.area())
21  rectangle.change_size(20, 40)
22  print(rectangle.area())
```

>> 200
>> 800

In this example, `Rectangle` objects have two instance variables: `len` and `width`. The `area` method returns the area of the `Rectangle` object by multiplying the instance variables together, and the `change_size` method changes them by assigning them to the numbers the caller passes in as parameters.

Object-oriented programming has several advantages. It encourages code reuse, and thus decreases the amount of time spent developing and maintaining code. It also encourages breaking problems up into multiple pieces, which results in code that is easy to maintain. A disadvantage of object-oriented programming is that creating programs takes extra effort because a great deal of planning is often involved in designing them.

Vocabulary

Programming paradigm: A style of programming.

State: The value of a program's variables while it is running.

Global state: The value of a program's global variables while it is running.

Procedural programming: A programming style in which you write a sequence of steps moving toward a solution—with each step changing the program's state.

Functional programming: Functional programming addresses the problems that arise in procedural programming by eliminating global state by passing it from function to function.

Side effect: Changing the state of a global variable.

Object-oriented: A programming paradigm where you define objects that interact with each other.

Classes: A mechanism allowing the programmer to classify and group together similar objects.

Methods: Methods are suites in a class. They are like functions, but you define them inside of a class, and you can only call them on the object the class creates.

Instance: Every object is an instance of a class. Every instance of a class has the same type as all the other instances of that class.

Instance variables: Variables that belong to an object.

Magic method: A method Python uses in different situations, like initializing an object.

Instantiating a class: Creating a new object using a class.

Challenges

1. Define a class called `Apple` with four instance variables that represent four attributes of an apple.

2. Create a `Circle` class with a method called `area` that calculates and returns its area. Then create a `Circle` object, call `area` on it, and print the result. Use Python's `pi` function in the built-in `math` module.

3. Create a `Triangle` class with a method called `area` that calculates and returns its area. Then create a `Triangle` object, call `area` on it, and print the result.

4. Make a `Hexagon` class with a method called `calculate_perimeter` that calculates and returns its perimeter. Then create a `Hexagon` object, call `calculate_perimeter` on it, and print the result.

Solutions: http://tinyurl.com/gpqe62e.

Chapter 13. The Four Pillars of Object-Oriented Programming

"Good design adds value faster than it adds cost."
—Thomas C. Gale

There are four main concepts in object-oriented programming: encapsulation, abstraction, polymorphism, and inheritance. Together, they form the **four pillars of object-oriented programming**. All four concepts must be present in a programming language for it to be considered a fully object-oriented programming language, like Python, Java, and Ruby. In this chapter, you will learn about each of the four pillars of object-oriented programming.

Encapsulation

Encapsulation refers to two concepts. The first is that in object-oriented programming, objects group variables (state) and methods (for altering state or doing calculations that use state) in a single unit—the object:

```
1
2   # http://tinyurl.com/j74o5rh
3
4
5   class Rectangle():
6       def __init__(self, w, l):
7           self.width = w
8           self.len = l
9
10
11      def area(self):
12          return self.width * self.len
```

In this case, the instance variables `len` and `width` hold the object's state. The object's state is grouped in the same unit (the object) as the method `area`. The method uses the object's state to return the rectangle's area.

The second concept, encapsulation, refers to hiding a class's internal data to prevent the **client**, the code outside the class that uses the object, from directly accessing it:

```
1   # http://tinyurl.com/jtz28ha
2
3
4   class Data:
5       def __init__(self):
6           self.nums = [1, 2, 3, 4, 5]
7
8
9       def change_data(self, index, n):
10          self.nums[index] = n
```

The class Data has an instance variable called nums that contains a list of integers. Once you create a Data object, there are two ways you can change the items in nums: by using the change_data method, or by directly accessing the nums instance variable using the Data object:

```
1   # http://tinyurl.com/huczqr5
2
3
4   class Data:
5       def __init__(self):
6           self.nums = [1, 2, 3, 4, 5]
7
8
9       def change_data(self, index, n):
10          self.nums[index] = n
11
12
13  data_one = Data()
14  data_one.nums[0] = 100
15  print(data_one.nums)
16
17
18  data_two = Data()
19  data_two.change_data(0, 100)
20  print(data_two.nums)
```

```
>> [100, 2, 3, 4, 5]
>> [100, 2, 3, 4, 5]
```

Both ways of changing an item in the nums instance variable work, but what happens if you decide to make the variable nums a tuple instead of a list? If you make this change, any client code trying to alter the items in the variable nums, like you did with nums[0] = 100, will no longer work, because tuples are immutable.

Many programming languages solve this problem by allowing programmers to define **private variables** and **private methods**: variables and methods that objects can access in the code that implements the various methods, but the client cannot. Private variables and methods are useful when you have a method or variable that your class uses internally, but you plan to change the implementation of your code later (or you want to preserve the flexibility of that option), and thus don't want whoever is using the class to rely on them because they might change (and would then break the client's code). Private variables are an example of the second concept encapsulation refers to; private variables hide a class's internal data to prevent the client from directly accessing it. **Public variables**, on the other hand, are variables a client can access.

Python does not have private variables. All of Python's variables are public. Python solves the problem private variables address another way—by using naming conventions. In Python, if you have a variable or method the caller should not access, you precede its name with an underscore. Python programmers know if the name of a method or variable starts with an underscore, they shouldn't use it (although they are still able to at their own risk):

```
1   # http://tinyurl.com/jkaorle
2
3
4   class PublicPrivateExample:
5       def __init__(self):
6           self.public = "safe"
7           self._unsafe = "unsafe"
8
9
10      def public_method(self):
11          # clients can use this
12          pass
13
14
15      def _unsafe_method(self):
16          # clients shouldn't use this
17          pass
```

Client programmers reading this code know the variable `self.public` is safe to use, but they shouldn't use the variable `self._unsafe` because it starts with an underscore, and if they do, they do so at their own risk. The person maintaining this code has no obligation to keep the variable `self._unsafe` around, because callers are a not supposed to be accessing it. Client programmers know the method `public_method` is safe to use, whereas the method `_unsafe_method` is not, because its name starts with an underscore.

Abstraction

Abstraction is the process of "taking away or removing characteristics from something in order to reduce it to a set of essential characteristics."[7] You use abstraction in object-oriented programming when you model objects using classes and omit unnecessary details.

Say you are modeling a person. A person is complex: they have a hair color, eye color, height, weight, ethnicity, gender, and more. If you create a class to represent a person, some of these details may not be relevant to the problem you are trying to solve. An example of abstraction is creating a `Person` class, but omitting some attributes a person has, like an eye color and height. The `Person` objects your class creates are abstractions of people. It is a representation of a person stripped down to only the essential characteristics necessary for the problem you are solving.

Polymorphism

Polymorphism is "the ability (in programming) to present the same interface for differing underlying forms (data types)."[8] An interface is a function or a method. Here is an example of presenting the same interface for different data types:

```
1  # http://tinyurl.com/hrxd7gn
2
3
4  print("Hello, World!")
5  print(200)
6  print(200.1)

>> Hello, World!
>> 200
>> 200.1
```

You presented the same interface, the `print` function, for three different data types: a string, an integer, and a floating-point number. You didn't have to define and call three separate functions (like `print_string` to print strings, `print_int` to print integers, and `print_float` to print floating-point numbers) to print three different data types; instead, you were able to use the `print` function to present one interface to print them all.

The built-in function `type` returns the data type of an object:

```
1  # http://tinyurl.com/gnxq24x
2
3
4  type("Hello, World!")
5  type(200)
6  type(200.1)

>> <class 'str'>
>> <class 'int'>
>> <class 'float'>
```

Let's say you want to write a program that creates three objects that draw themselves: triangles, squares, and circles. You can achieve this goal by defining three different classes: `Triangle`, `Square`, and `Circle`, and defining a method called `draw` for each of them. `Triangle.draw()` will draw a triangle. `Square.draw()` will draw a square. And `Circle.draw()` will draw a circle. With this design, each of the objects has a `draw` interface that knows how to draw itself. You presented the same interface for three different data types.

If Python did not support polymorphism, you would need a method to draw each shape: perhaps `draw_triangle` to draw a `Triangle` object, `draw_square` to draw a `Square` object, and `draw_circle` to draw a `Circle` object.

Also, if you had a list of these objects and you wanted to draw each one, you would have to test each object to get its type, then call the correct method for that type, making the program larger, harder to read, harder to write, and more fragile. It also makes the program harder to enhance, because every time you added a new shape to your program, you would have to track down every place in the code where you draw the shapes and add a test (to find what method to use) for that new shape type, plus a call to that new draw function. Here is an example of drawing shapes with and without polymorphism:

```
1  # Do not run.
2
3
4
5  # Drawing shapes
6  # w/o polymorphism
7  shapes = [tr1, sq1, cr1]
8  for a_shape in shapes:
9      if type(a_shape) == "Triangle":
10         a_shape.draw_triangle()
11     if type(a_shape) == "Square":
12         a_shape.draw_square()
13     if type(a_shape) == "Circle":
14         a_shape.draw_circle()
15
16
17 # Drawing shapes
18 # with polymorphism
19 shapes = [tr1,
20           sw1,
21           cr1]
22 for a_shape in shapes:
23     a_shape.draw()
```

If you wanted to add a new shape to the shapes list without polymorphism, you would have to modify the code in the for-loop to test a_shape type and call its draw method. With a uniform, polymorphic interface, you can add as many shape classes to the shapes list in the future as you want, and the shape will be able to draw itself without any additional code.

Inheritance

Inheritance in programming is similar to genetic inheritance. In genetic inheritance, you inherit attributes like eye color from your parents. Similarly, when you create a class, it can inherit methods and variables from another class. The class that is inherited from is the **parent class**, and the class that inherits is the **child class**. In this section, you will model shapes using inheritance. Here is a class that models a shape:

```
1  # http://tinyurl.com/zrnqeo3
2
3
4  class Shape():
5      def __init__(self, w, l):
6          self.width = w
7          self.len = l
8
9
10     def print_size(self):
11         print("""{} by {}
12                """.format(self.width,
13                           self.len))
14
15
16 my_shape = Shape(20, 25)
17 my_shape.print_size()
```

>> 20 by 25

With this class, you can create Shape objects with width and len. In addition, Shape objects have the method print_size, which prints their width and len.

You can define a child class that inherits from a parent class by passing the name of the parent class as a parameter to the child class when you create it. The following example creates a Square class that inherits from the Shape class:

```
 1  # http://tinyurl.com/j81j35s
 2
 3
 4  class Shape():
 5      def __init__(self, w, l):
 6          self.width = w
 7          self.len = l
 8
 9
10      def print_size(self):
11          print("""{} by {}
12                  """.format(self.width,
13                                  self.len))
14
15
16  class Square(Shape):
17      pass
18
19
20  a_square = Square(20,20)
21  a_square.print_size()
```

>> 20 by 20

Because you passed the Shape class to the Square class as a parameter; the Square class inherits the Shape class's variables and methods. The only suite you defined in the Square class was the keyword pass, which tells Python not to do anything.

Because of inheritance, you can create a Square object, pass it a width and length, and call the method print_size on it without writing any code (aside from pass) in the Square class. This reduction in code is important because avoiding repeating code makes your program smaller and more manageable.

A child class is like any other class; you can define methods and variables in it without affecting the parent class:

```
 1  # http://tinyurl.com/hwjdcy9
 2
 3
 4  class Shape():
 5      def __init__(self, w, l):
 6          self.width = w
 7          self.len = l
 8
 9
10      def print_size(self):
11          print("""{} by {}
12              """.format(self.width,
13                          self.len))
14
15
16  class Square(Shape):
17      def area(self):
18          return self.width * self.len
19
20
21  a_square = Square(20, 20)
22  print(a_square.area())
```

>> 400

When a child class inherits a method from a parent class, you can override it by defining a new method with the same name as the inherited method. A child class's ability to change the implementation of a method inherited from its parent class is called **method overriding**.

```
1  # http://tinyurl.com/hy9m8ht
2
3
4  class Shape():
5      def __init__(self, w, l):
6          self.width = w
7          self.len = l
8
9
10     def print_size(self):
11         print("""{} by {}
12                """.format(self.width,
13                           self.len))
14
15
16 class Square(Shape):
17     def area(self):
18         return self.width * self.len
19
20
21     def print_size(self):
22         print("""I am {} by {}
23                """.format(self.width,
24                           self.len))
25
26
27 a_square = Square(20, 20)
28 a_square.print_size()
```

```
>> I am 20 by 20
```

In this case, because you defined a method named `print_size`, the newly defined method overrides the parent method of the same name, and it prints a new message when you call it.

Composition

Now that you've learned about the four pillars of object-oriented programming, I am going to cover one more important concept: **composition**. Composition models the "has a" relationship by storing an object as a variable in another object. For example, you can use composition to represent the relationship between a dog and its owner (a dog has an owner). To model this, first you define classes to represent dogs and people:

```
1  # http://tinyurl.com/zqg488n
2
3
4  class Dog():
5      def __init__(self,
6                       name,
7                       breed,
8          owner):
9          self.name = name
10         self.breed = breed
11         self.owner = owner
12
13
14 class Person():
15     def __init__(self, name):
16         self.name = name
```

Then, when you create a Dog object, you pass in a Person object as the owner parameter:

```
1  # http://tinyurl.com/zlzefd4
2  # Continue from
3  # last example
4
5
6  mick = Person("Mick Jagger")
7  stan = Dog("Stanley",
8             "Bulldog",
9             mick)
10 print(stan.owner.name)
```

>> Mick Jagger

Now the stan object "Stanley" has an owner—a Person object named "Mick Jagger"—stored in the owner instance variable.

Vocabulary

The four pillars of object-oriented programming: The four main concepts in object-oriented programming: inheritance, polymorphism, abstraction, and encapsulation.
Inheritance: In genetic inheritance, you inherit attributes like eye color from your parents. Similarly, when you create a class, it can inherit methods and variables from another class. **Parent class**: The class that is inherited from.
Child class: The class that inherits.
Method overriding: A child class's ability to change the implementation of a method inherited from its parent class.
Polymorphism: Polymorphism is "the ability (in programming) to present the same interface for differing underlying forms (data types)."[9]
Abstraction: The process of "taking away or removing characteristics from something in order to reduce it to a set of essential characteristics."[10]
Client: The code outside the class that uses the object.
Encapsulation: Encapsulation refers to two concepts. The first concept is that in object-oriented programming, objects group variables (state) and methods (for altering state) in a single unit—the object. The second concept is hiding a class's internal data to prevent the client, the person using the code, from accessing it.
Composition: Composition models the "has a" relationship by storing an object as a variable in another object.

Challenges

1. Create `Rectangle` and `Square` classes with a method called `calculate_perimeter` that calculates the perimeter of the shapes they represent. Create `Rectangle` and `Square` objects and call the method on both of them.
2. Define a method in your `Square` class called `change_size` that allows you to pass in a number that increases or decreases (if the number is negative) each side of a `Square` object by that number.
3. Create a class called `Shape`. Define a method in it called `what_am_i` that prints "I am a shape" when called. Change your `Square` and `Rectangle` classes from the previous challenges to inherit from `Shape`, create `Square` and `Rectangle` objects, and call the new method on both of them.
4. Create a class called `Horse` and a class called `Rider`. Use composition to model a horse that has a rider.

Solutions: http://tinyurl.com/hz9qdh3.

Chapter 14. More Object-Oriented Programming

"Treat your code like poetry and take it to the edge of the bare minimum."
—Ilya Dorman

In this chapter, I cover additional concepts related to object-oriented programming.

Class Variables vs. Instance Variables

In Python, classes are objects. This idea comes from Smalltalk, an influential programming language that pioneered object-oriented programming. Each class in Python is an object that is an instance of class "type":

```
1  # http://tinyurl.com/h7ypzmd
2
3
4  class Square:
5      pass
6
7
8  print(Square)
```

```
>> <class '__main__.Square'>
```

In this example, the class `Square` is an object, and you printed it.

Classes have two types of variables: **class variables** and **instance variables.** The variables you've seen so far have been instance variables, defined with the syntax `self.[variable_name] = [variable_value]`. Instance variables belong to objects:

```
1   # http://tinyurl.com/zmnf47e
2
3
4   class Rectangle():
5       def __init__(self, w, l):
6           self.width = w
7           self.len = l
8
9
10      def print_size(self):
11          print("""{} by {}
12                """.format(self.width,
13                              self.len))
14
15
16  my_rectangle = Rectangle(10, 24)
17  my_rectangle.print_size()
```

>> 10 by 24

In this example, width and len are instance variables.

Class variables belong to the object Python creates for each class definition and the objects they create. You define class variables like regular variables (but you must define them inside of a class). You can access them with class objects, and with an object created with a class object. You access them the same way you access instance variables (preceding the variable name with self.). Class variables are useful; they allow you to share data between all of the instances of a class without relying on global variables:

```
 1  # http://tinyurl.com/gu9unfc
 2
 3
 4  class Rectangle():
 5      recs = []
 6
 7
 8      def __init__(self, w, l):
 9          self.width = w
10          self.len = l
11          self.recs.append((self.width,
12                                  self.len))
13
14
15      def print_size(self):
16          print("""{} by {}
17              """.format(self.width,
18                                  self.len))
19
20
21  r1 = Rectangle(10, 24)
22  r2 = Rectangle(20, 40)
23  r3 = Rectangle(100, 200)
24
25
26  print(Rectangle.recs)
```

>> [(10, 24), (20, 40), (100, 200)]

In this example, you added a class variable called recs to the Rectangle class. You defined it outside of the __init__ method because Python only calls the __init__ method when you create an object, and you want to be able to access the class variable using the class object (which does not call the __init__ method).

Next, you created three Rectangle objects. Each time a Rectangle object is created, the code in the __init__ method appends a tuple containing the width and length of the newly created object to the recs list. With this code, whenever you create a new Rectangle object, it is automatically added to the recs list. By using a class variable, you were able to share data between the different objects created by a class, without having to use a global variable.

Magic Methods

Every class in Python inherits from a parent class called Object. Python utilizes the methods inherited from Object in different situations—like when you print an object:

```
1   # http://tinyurl.com/ze8yr7s
2
3
4   class Lion:
5       def __init__(self, name):
6           self.name = name
7
8
9   lion = Lion("Dilbert")
10  print(lion)
```

>> <__main__.Lion object at 0x101178828>

When you print a Lion object, Python calls a magic method called __repr__ it inherited from Object on it, and prints whatever the __repr__ method returns. You can override the inherited __repr__ method to change what prints:

```
1   # http://tinyurl.com/j5rocqm
2
3
4   class Lion:
5       def __init__(self, name):
6           self.name = name
7
8
9       def __repr__(self):
10          return self.name
11
12
13  lion = Lion("Dilbert")
14  print(lion)
```

>> Dilbert

Because you overrode the __repr__ method inherited from Object and changed it to return the Lion object's name, when you print a Lion object, its name— in this case, Dilbert— prints instead of something like <__main__.Lion object at 0x101178828> that the __repr__ method would have returned.

Operands in an expression must have a magic method the operator can use to evaluate the expression. For example, in the expression 2 + 2, each integer object has a magic method called __add__ that Python calls when it evaluates the expression. If you define an __add__ method in a class, you can use the objects it creates as operands in an expression with the addition operator:

```
1   # http://tinyurl.com/hlmhrwv
2
3
4   class AlwaysPositive:
5       def __init__(self, number):
6           self.n = number
7
8
9       def __add__(self, other):
10          return abs(self.n +
11                      other.n)
12
13
14  x = AlwaysPositive(-20)
15  y = AlwaysPositive(10)
16
17
18  print(x + y)
```

>> 10

AlwaysPositive objects can be used as operands in an expression with the addition operator because you defined the __add__ method. When Python evaluates an expression with an addition operator, it calls the method __add__ on the first operand object, passes the second operand object into __add__ as a parameter, and returns the result.

In this case, __add__ uses the built-in function abs to return the absolute value of two numbers added together in an expression. Because you defined __add__ this way, two AlwaysPositive objects evaluated in an expression with the addition operator will always return the absolute value of the sum of the two objects; thus, the result of the expression is always positive.

Is

The keyword is returns True if two objects are the same object, and False if not:

```
1   # http://tinyurl.com/gt28gww
2
3
4   class Person:
5       def __init__(self):
6           self.name = 'Bob'
7
8
9   bob = Person()
10  same_bob = bob
11  print(bob is same_bob)
12
13
14  another_bob = Person()
15  print(bob is another_bob)
```

```
>> True
>> False
```

When you use the keyword is in an expression with the objects bob and same_bob as operators, the expression evaluates to True because both variables point to the same Person object. When you create a new Person object and compare it to the original bob, the expression evaluates to False because the variables point to different Person objects.

Use the is keyword to check if a variable is None:

```
1  # http://tinyurl.com/jjettn2
2
3
4  x = 10
5  if x is None:
6      print("x is None :( ")
7  else:
8      print("x is not None")
9
10
11 x = None
12 if x is None:
13     print("x is None :(")
14 else:
15     print("x is not None")

>> x is not None
>> x is None :(
```

Vocabulary

Class variable: A class variable belongs to a class object and the objects it creates.
Instance variable: An instance variable belongs to an object.
Private variables: A variable an object can access, but the client cannot.
Private method: A method an object can access, but the client cannot.
Public variable: A variable a client can access.

Challenges

1. Add a `square_list` class variable to a class called `Square` so that every time you create a new `Square` object, the new object gets added to the list.
2. Change the `Square` class so that when you print a `Square` object, a message prints telling you the len of each of the four sides of the shape. For example, if you create a square with `Square(29)` and print it, Python should print `29 by 29 by 29 by 29`.
3. Write a function that takes two objects as parameters and returns `True` if they are the same object, and `False` if not.

Solutions: http://tinyurl.com/j9qjnep.

Chapter 15. Bringing It All Together

"It's all talk until the code runs."
—Ward Cunningham

In this chapter, you are going to create the popular card game War. In War, each player draws a card from the deck, and the player with the highest card wins. You will build War by defining classes representing a card, a deck, a player, and finally, the game itself.

Cards

Here is a class that models playing cards:

```
1   # http://tinyurl.com/jj22qv4
2
3
4   class Card:
5       suits = ("spades",
6               "hearts",
7               "diamonds",
8               "clubs")
9
10
11      values = (None, None,"2", "3",
12              "4", "5", "6", "7",
13              "8", "9", "10",
14              "Jack", "Queen",
15              "King", "Ace")
16
17
18      def __init__(self, v, s):
19          """suit + value are ints"""
20          self.value = v
21          self.suit = s
22
23
24      def __lt__(self, c2):
25          if self.value < c2.value:
26              return True
```

```
27          if self.value == c2.value:
28              if self.suit < c2.suit:
29                  return True
30              else:
31                  return False
32          return False
33
34
35      def __lt__(self, c2):
36          if self.value > c2.value:
37              return True
38          if self.value == c2.value:
39              if self.suit > c2.suit:
40                  return True
41              else:
42                  return False
43          return False
44
45
46      def __repr__(self):
47          v = self.values[self.value] + " of " \
48              + self.suits[self.suit]
49          return v
```

The Card class has two class variables, suits and values. suits is a tuple of strings representing all the suits a card could be: spades, hearts, diamonds, clubs. values is a tuple of strings representing the different numeric values a card could be: 2-10, Jack, Queen, King and Ace. The items at the first two indexes of the values tuple are None, so that the strings in the tuple match up with the index they represent—so the string "2" in the values tuple is at index 2.

Card objects have two instance variables: suit and value—each represented by an integer. Together, the instance variables represent what kind of card the Card object is. For example, you create a 2 of hearts by creating a Card object and passing it the parameters 2 (for the suit) and 1 (for the value—1 because hearts is at index 1 in the suits tuple).

The definitions in the magic methods __lt__ and __gt__ allow you to c ompare t wo Card objects in an expression using the greater than and less than operators. The code in these methods determines if the card is greater than or less than the other card passed in as a parameter. The code in these magic methods can also handle if the cards have the same value—for example if both cards are 10s. If this occurs, the methods use the value of the suits to break the tie. The suits are arranged in order of strength in the `suits` tuple—with the strongest suit last, and thus assigned the highest index, and the least powerful suit assigned the lowest index.

```
1  # http://tinyurl.com/j6donnr
2
3
4  card1 = Card(10, 2)
5  card2 = Card(11, 3)
6  print(card1 < card2)
```

>> True

```
1  # http://tinyurl.com/hc9ktlr
2
3
4  card1 = Card(10, 2)
5  card2 = Card(11, 3)
6  print(card1 > card2)
```

>> False

The last method in the `Card` class is the magic method `__repr__`. Its code uses the `value` and `suit` instance variables to look up the value and suit of the card in the `values` and `suits` tuples, and returns them so you can print the card a `Card` object represents:

```
1  # http://tinyurl.com/z57hc75
2
3
4  card = Card(3, 2)
5  print(card)
```

>> 3 of diamonds

Deck

Next, you need to define a class to represent a deck of cards:

```
1   # http://tinyurl.com/jz8zfz7
2   from random import shuffle
3
4
5   class Deck:
6       def __init__(self):
7           self.cards = []
8           for i in range(2, 15):
9               for j in range(4):
10                  self.cards.append(Card(i, j))
11          shuffle(self.cards)
12
13
14      def rm_card(self):
15          if len(self.cards) == 0:
16              return
17          return self.cards.pop()
```

When you initialize the Deck object, the two for-loops in __init__ create Card objects representing all the cards in a 52-card deck and appends them to the cards list. The first loop is from 2 to 15 because the first value for a card is 2, and the last value for a card is 14 (the ace). Each time around the inner loop, a new card is created using the integer from the outer loop as the value (i.e., 14 for an ace) and the integer from the inner loop as the suit (i.e. a 2 for hearts). This process creates 52 cards—one card for every suit and value combination. After the method creates the cards, the shuffle method from the random module randomly rearranges the items in the cards list; mimicking the shuffling of a deck of cards.

Our deck has one other method called rm_card that removes and returns a card from the cards list, or returns None if it is empty. You can use the Deck class to create a new deck of cards and print each card in it:

```
1   # http://tinyurl.com/hsv5n6p
2
3
4   deck = Deck()
5   for card in deck.cards:
6       print(card)
```

```
>> 4 of spades
>> 8 of hearts
```

...

Player

You need a class to represent each player in the game to keep track of their cards and how many rounds they've won:

```
1   # http://tinyurl.com/gwyrt2s
2
3
4   class Player:
5       def __init__(self, name):
6           self.wins = 0
7           self.card = None
8           self.name = name
```

The Player class has three instance variables: wins to keep track of how many rounds a player has won, card to represent the card a player is currently holding, and name to keep track of a player's name.

Game

Finally, you need a class to represent the game:

```
1   # http://tinyurl.com/huwq8mw
2
3
4   class Game:
5       def __init__(self):
6           name1 = input("p1 name ")
7           name2 = input("p2 name ")
8           self.deck = Deck()
9           self.p1 = Player(name1)
10          self.p2 = Player(name2)
11
12
13      def wins(self, winner):
14          w = "{} wins this round"
15          w = w.format(winner)
16          print(w)
17
```

```
18
19      def draw(self, p1n, p1c, p2n, p2c):
20          d = "{} drew {} {} drew {}"
21          d = d.format(p1n, p1c, p2n, p2c)
22          print(d)
23
24
25      def play_game(self):
26          cards = self.deck.cards
27          print("beginning War!")
28          while len(cards) >= 2:
29              m = "q to quit. Any " + "key to play:"
30              response = input(m)
31              if response == 'q':
32                  break
33              p1c = self.deck.rm_card()
34              p2c = self.deck.rm_card()
35              p1n = self.p1.name
36              p2n = self.p2.name
37              self.draw(p1n, p1c, p2n, p2c)
38              if p1c > p2c:
39                  self.p1.wins += 1
40                  self.wins(self.p1.name)
41              else:
42                  self.p2.wins += 1
43                  self.wins(self.p2.name)
44
45
46          win = self.winner(self.p1, self.p2)
47
48          print("War is over.{} wins".format(win))
49
50
51      def winner(self, p1, p2):
52          if p1.wins > p2.wins:
53              return p1.name
54          if p1.wins < p2.wins:
55              return p2.name
56          return "It was a tie!"
```

When you create the game object, Python calls the __init__ method, and the input function collects the names of the two players in the game and stores them in the variables name1 and name2. Next, you create a new Deck object, store it in the instance variable deck, and create two Player objects using the names in name1 and name2.

The method play_game in the Game class starts the game. There is a loop in the method that keeps the game going as long as there are two or more cards left in the deck, and as long as the variable response does not equal q. Each time around the loop, you assign the variable response to the input of the user. The game continues until either the user types "q", or when there are less than two cards left in the deck.

Two cards are drawn each time through the loop, and the play_game method assigns the first card to p1, and the second card to p2. Then, it prints the name of each player and the card they drew, compares the two cards to see which card is greater, increments the wins instance variable for the player with the greater card, and prints a message that says who won.

The Game class also has a method called winner that takes two player objects, looks at the number of rounds they won, and returns the player who won the most rounds.

When the Deck object runs out of cards, the play_game method prints a message saying the war is over, calls the winner method (passing in both p1 and p2), and prints a message with the result—the name of the player who won.

War

Here is the full game:

```
1   # http://tinyurl.com/ho7364a
2
3
4   from random import shuffle
5
6
7   class Card:
8       suits = ["spades",
9                "hearts",
10               "diamonds",
11               "clubs"]
12
13
14       values = [None, None,"2", "3",
```

```
15              "4", "5", "6", "7",
16              "8", "9", "10",
17              "Jack", "Queen",
18              "King", "Ace"]
19
20
21      def __init__(self, v, s):
22          """suit + value are ints"""
23          self.value = v
24          self.suit = s
25
26
27      def __lt__(self, c2):
28          if self.value < c2.value:
29              return True
30          if self.value == c2.value:
31              if self.suit < c2.suit:
32                  return True
33              else:
34                  return False
35          return False
36
37
38      def __gt__(self, c2):
39          if self.value > c2.value:
40              return True
41          if self.value == c2.value:
42              if self.suit > c2.suit:
43                  return True
44              else:
45                  return False
46          return False
47
48
49      def __repr__(self):
50          v = self.values[self.value] + " of " \
51          + self.suits[self.suit]
52          return v
53
54
55  class Deck:
```

```
56        def __init__(self):
57            self.cards = []
58            for i in range(2, 15):
59                for j in range(4):
60                    self.cards.append(Card(i, j))
61            shuffle(self.cards)
62
63
64        def rm_card(self):
65            if len(self.cards) == 0:
66                return
67            return self.cards.pop()
68
69
70    class Player:
71        def __init__(self, name):
72            self.wins = 0
73            self.card = None
74            self.name = name
75
76
77    class Game:
78        def __init__(self):
79            name1 = input("p1 name ")
80            name2 = input("p2 name ")
81            self.deck = Deck()
82            self.p1 = Player(name1)
83            self.p2 = Player(name2)
84
85
86        def wins(self, winner):
87            w = "{} wins this round"
88            w = w.format(winner)
89            print(w)
90
91
92        def draw(self, p1n, p1c, p2n, p2c):
93            d = "{} drew {} {} drew {}"
94            d = d.format(p1n, p1c, p2n, p2c)
95            print(d)
96
```

```
 97
 98        def play_game(self):
 99            cards = self.deck.cards
100            print("beginning War!")
101            while len(cards) >= 2:
102                m = "q to quit. Any " + "key to play:"
103                response = input(m)
104                if response == 'q':
105                    break
106                p1c = self.deck.rm_card()
107                p2c = self.deck.rm_card()
108                p1n = self.p1.name
109                p2n = self.p2.name
110                self.draw(p1n, p1c, p2n, p2c)
111                if p1c > p2c:
112                    self.p1.wins += 1
113                    self.wins(self.p1.name)
114                else:
115                    self.p2.wins += 1
116                    self.wins(self.p2.name)
117
118
119            win = self.winner(self.p1, self.p2)
120
121            print("War is over.{} wins".format(win))
122
123
124        def winner(self, p1, p2):
125            if p1.wins > p2.wins:
126                return p1.name
127            if p1.wins < p2.wins:
128                return p2.name
129            return "It was a tie!"
130
131
132    game = Game()
133    game.play_game()

>> "p1 name "
...
```

Part III
Introduction to Programming Tools

Chapter 16. Bash

"I can't think of a job I'd rather do than computer programming. All day, you create patterns and structure out of the formless void, and you solve dozens of smaller puzzles along the way."
—Peter Van Der Linden

In this chapter, you learn to use a **command-line interface** called **Bash**. A command-line interface is a program you type instructions into that your operating system executes. Bash is a particular implementation of a command-line interface that comes with most Unix-like operating systems. Henceforth, I will use command-line interface and **command-line** interchangeably.

When I got my first programming job, I made the mistake of spending all of my time practicing programming. Of course, you need to be a talented programmer to program professionally. But there are also a variety of other skills you need to have, like knowing how to use the command-line. The command-line is the "control center" for everything you will be doing that doesn't involve writing code.

For instance, later in this book you will learn to use package managers to install other people's programs and version control systems to collaborate with other programmers. You will operate both of these tools from the command-line. Furthermore, most software written today involves accessing data across the Internet, and the majority of the world's web servers run Linux. These servers do not have a user interface; you can only access them via the command-line.

The command-line, package managers, regular expressions and version control are core tools in a programmer's arsenal. Everyone on the teams I've worked on has been an expert at these things.

When you program professionally, you will be expected to be proficient with them as well. It took me a long time to catch up, and I wish I had started learning to use these tools earlier.

Following Along

If you are using either Ubuntu or Unix, your computer comes with Bash. Windows, however, comes with a command-line interface called **Command Prompt** (which you cannot use in this chapter). The newest version of Windows 10 comes with Bash. You can find instructions on how to use Bash on Windows 10 at http://theselftaughtprogrammer.io/windows10bash.

If you are using Windows, you can use Amazon AWS to set up a free web server running Ubuntu. Setting up a server is easy, and AWS is widely used in the programing world, so it will give you valuable experience. Head to http://theselftaughtprogrammer.io/aws to get started.

If you are using Windows, and you do not want to set up a server, you can follow along with the examples by going to http://theselftaughtprogrammer.io/bashapp, where you will find a link to a web app that emulates Bash that you can use to follow along with most of the examples.

After this chapter, you can follow along with the examples in the next two chapters using Windows Command Prompt. You can find it by searching for `Command Prompt` from the `Run Window`.

Finding Bash

You can find Bash on your computer by searching for `Terminal` from the icon titled `Search your computer and online resources` if you are using Ubuntu, or from `Spotlight search` if you are using a Mac.

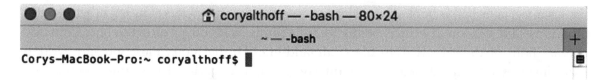

Commands

Bash is similar to the Python Shell. You type commands, which are like functions in Python, into Bash. Then you type a space and the parameters you want to pass to the command (if any). Hit the enter key, and Bash returns the result. The command `echo` is similar to the `print` function in Python.

Whenever you see a dollar sign followed by a command, in either this book or in programming documentation, it means you need to type the command into the command-line:

```
# http://tinyurl.com/junx62n

$ echo Hello, World!
```

```
   >> Hello, World!
```

First, you typed the command `echo` into Bash, followed by a space and `Hello, World!` as a parameter. When you press enter, `Hello, World!` prints in Bash.

You can use programs you've installed, like Python, from the command-line. Enter the command `python3` (As I am writing, the Bash Web App doesn't come with Python 3. Type `python` to use Python 2):

```
# http://tinyurl.com/htoospk

$ python3
```

Now you can execute Python code:

```
# http://tinyurl.com/jk2acua

print("Hello, World!")
```

```
   >> Hello, World!
```

Enter `exit()` to exit Python.

Recent Commands

You can scroll through your recent commands by pressing the up and down arrows in Bash. To see a list of all of your recent commands use the command `history`:

```
# http://tinyurl.com/go2spbt

$ history
```

```
   >> 1. echo Hello, World!
```

Relative vs. Absolute Paths

An operating system is made up of directories and files. A **directory** is another word for a folder on your computer. All directories and files have a path, an address where the directory or file exists in your operating system. When you use Bash, you are always in a directory, located at a particular path. You can use the command `pwd`, which stands for print **working directory** (your working directory is the directory you are currently in), to print the name of the directory you are in:

```
# http://tinyurl.com/hptsqhp

$ pwd
```

>> /Users/coryalthoff

Your operating system represents its directories, and your directory location, with a tree. In computer science, a tree is an important concept called a data structure (covered in Part IV). In a tree, there is a root at the top. The root can have branches, and each one of the branches can have more branches, and those branches can have branches, ad infinitum. The following image is an example of a tree that represents the directories in an operating system:

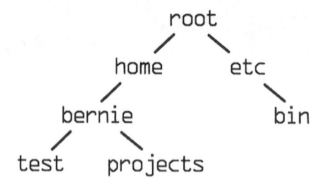

Every branch of the tree is a directory, including the root. The tree shows how the directories connect to each other. Whenever you are using Bash, you are at a location on your operating system's tree. A **path** is a way of expressing that location. There are two ways to give the path of a file or directory on a Unix-like operating system: an **absolute path** and a **relative path**.

An absolute path gives the location of a file or directory starting from the root directory. An absolute path is made up of the name of directories in the tree, in order of their proximity to the tree's root, separated by forward slashes. The absolute path to the bernie directory (in the operating system illustrated in the image above) is /home/bernie. The first slash represents the root directory. The home directory follows it. Then there is another slash and the bernie directory.

Another way of specifying a location on your computer is a relative path. Instead of starting at the root directory, a relative path starts with your current working directory. If your path does not begin with a forward slash, Bash knows you are using a relative path. If you were in the home directory in the image of a tree from the previous example, the relative path to the projects directory would be bernie/projects. If you were in the home directory, the relative path to bernie is simply bernie. If you were in the root directory, the relative path to projects would be home/bernie/projects.

Navigating

You can change directories by passing the command cd an absolute or relative path as a parameter. Enter the cd command followed by the absolute path / to navigate to your operating system's root directory:

```
# http://tinyurl.com/hjgz79h

$ cd /
```

You can verify your location with the command pwd:

```
# http://tinyurl.com/j6ax35s

$ pwd
```

```
>> /
```

The list directory command, ls, prints the directories and folders in your current working directory:

```
# http://tinyurl.com/gw4d5yw

$ ls
```

```
>> bin dev initrd.img lost+found ...
```

You can create a new directory by passing in the name of the directory you want to create to the make directory command, mkdir. Directory names cannot have spaces in them. Navigate to your home directory (~ is a shortcut for your home directory in Unix-like operating systems) and use the mkdir command to create a new directory called tstp:

```
# http://tinyurl.com/zavhjeq

$ cd ~
$ mkdir tstp
```

You can verify your location with the command `ls`:

```
# http://tinyurl.com/hneq2f6

$ ls
```

```
>> tstp
```

Now, use the `cd` command to enter the `tstp` directory by passing it the relative path to `tstp` as a parameter:

```
# http://tinyurl.com/zp3nb2l

$ cd tstp
```

You can use the `cd` command followed by two periods to move back one directory (one level up the tree):

```
# http://tinyurl.com/z2gevk2

$ cd ..
```

You can delete a directory with the remove directory command, `rmdir`. Use it to remove the directory `tstp`:

```
# http://tinyurl.com/jkjjo6s

$ rmdir tstp
```

Finally, verify that you deleted the directory with the `ls` command.

```
# http://tinyurl.com/z32xn2n

$ ls
```

Flags

Commands have a concept called flags that allow the issuer of the command to change the command's behavior. Flags are options for commands that can have a value of either `True` or `False`. By default, all of a command's flags start set to `False`. If you add a flag to a command, Bash sets the value of the flag to `True` and the behavior of the command changes. To set a flag to `True`, you put one `(-)` or two `(--)` hyphen symbols in front of the name of the flag (depending on the operating system).

For example, you can add the flag `--author` to the `ls` command to set the `author` flag to `True`. Adding this flag to the `ls` command alters its behavior. When you add this flag to the `ls` command, it prints all of the directories and files in a directory, but also prints the name of the author, the person that created them.

On Unix, you use one hyphen in front of a flag:

```
# http://tinyurl.com/j4y5kz4

$ ls -author
```

```
>> drwx-------+ 13 coryalthoff 442B Sep 16 17:25 Pictures
>> drwx-------+ 25 coryalthoff 850B Nov 23 18:09 Documents
```

And on Linux you use two:

```
# http://tinyurl.com/hu9c54q

$ ls --author
```

```
>> drwx-------+ 13 coryalthoff 442B Sep 16 17:25 Pictures
>> drwx-------+ 25 coryalthoff 850B Nov 23 18:09 Documents
```

Hidden Files

Your operating system and many programs on your computer store data in hidden files. Hidden files are files that, by default, are not shown to users because changing them could affect the programs that depend on them. Hidden files start with a period, for example, .hidden. You can view hidden files by adding the flag -a, which stands for all, to the ls command. The command touch creates a new file from the command line.

The touch command creates a new file. Use it to create a hidden file named .self_taught:

```
# http://tinyurl.com/hfawo8t

$ touch .self_taught
```

Test if you can see it with the commands ls and ls -a.

pipes

In Unix-like operating systems, the vertical bar character (|) is called a **pipe**. You can use a pipe to pass the output of a command to another command as its input. For example, you can use the output of the ls command as the input of the less command (make sure you are not in an empty directory):

```
# http://tinyurl.com/zjne9f5

$ ls | less
```

```
>> Applications ...
```

The result is a text file with the output of ls opened up in the program less (press q to quit less).

Environmental Variables

Environmental variables are variables, stored in your operating system, that programs can use to get data about the environment they are running in such as the name of the computer the program is running on or the name of the operating system user running the program. You can create a new environmental variable in Bash with the syntax export variable_name=[variable_value]. To reference an environmental variable in Bash, you must put a dollar sign in front of its name:

```
# http://tinyurl.com/jjbc9v2

$ export x=100
$ echo $x
```

>> 100

An environmental variable created like this only exists in the Bash window you created it in. If you exit the Bash window you created the environmental variable in, reopen it and type echo $x, Bash will no longer print 100 because the environmental variable x no longer exists.

You can persist an environmental variable by adding it to a hidden file used by Unix-like operating systems, located in your home directory, called .profile. Use your GUI to navigate to your home directory. You can find the file path to your home directory from the command line with pwd ~. Use a text editor to create a file called .profile. Type export x=100 into the first line of the file, and save the file. Close and reopen Bash, and you should be able to print the environmental variable x:

```
# http://tinyurl.com/j5wjwdf

$ echo $x
```

>> 100

The variable will persist as long as it's in your .profile file. You can delete the variable by removing it from your .profile file.

Users

Operating systems can have multiple users. A user is a person that uses the operating system. Each user is assigned a username and password, which enables them to log in and use the operating system. Each user also has a set of permissions: operations they are allowed to perform. You can print the name of your operating system user with the command whoami (the examples in this section will not work on Bash on Windows or the Bash web app) :

```
1 | $ whoami
```

>> coryalthoff

Normally, you are the user you created when you installed your operating system. But this user is not the most powerful user in your operating system. The highest-level user, who is the user with the highest set of permissions, is called the root user. Every system has a root user who can, for example, create and delete other users.

For security reasons, you usually do not log in as the root user. Instead, you precede commands that you need to issue as the root user with the command `sudo` (superuser do). `sudo` allows you to issue commands as the root user without compromising your system's security by actually logging in as the root user. Here is an example of using the `echo` command with `sudo`:

```
$ sudo echo Hello, World!
```

```
>> Hello, World!
```

If you've set up a password on your computer, you will be prompted for it when you issue a command with `sudo`. `sudo` removes the safeguards that prevent you from harming your operating system, so never issue a command with `sudo` unless you are confident the command will not damage your operating system.

Learn More

I only covered the basics of Bash in this chapter. To learn more about using Bash, visit http://theselftaughtprogrammer.io/bash.

Vocabulary

Command-line interface: A command-line interface is a program you type instructions into that your operating system executes.
Command-line: Another name for a command-line interface.
Bash: A program that comes with most Unix-like operating systems that you type instructions into and your operating system executes.
Command prompt: A command-line interface that comes with Windows.
Directory: Another word for a folder on your computer.
Working directory: The directory you are currently in.
Path: A way of expressing the location in your operating system of a file or directory.
Absolute path: The location of a file or directory starting from the root directory.
Relative path: The location of a file or directory starting from your current working directory.

Pipe: The character | . On Unix-like operating systems, you can use a pipe to pass the output of a command to another command as its input.

Environmental variables: Variables that your operating system and other programs store data in.

$PATH: When you type a command into the Bash command shell, it looks for the command in all the directories stored in an environmental variable named $PATH.

User: A person that uses the operating system.

Permissions: Operations operating system users are allowed to do.

Root user: The highest-level user, the user with the highest set of permissions.

Challenges

1. Print Self-taught in Bash.
2. Navigate to your home directory from another directory using an absolute and relative path.
3. Create an environmental variable called $python_projects that is an absolute path to the directory where you keep your Python files. Save the variable in your .profile file and then use the command cd $python_projects to navigate there.

Solutions: http://tinyurl.com/zdeyg8y.

Chapter 17. Regular Expressions

"Talk is cheap. Show me the code."
—Linus Torvalds

Many programming languages and operating systems support **regular expressions**: a "sequence of characters that define a search pattern."[11] Regular expressions are helpful because you can use them to search a file or other data for a complex pattern. For example, you can use a regular expression to match all of the numbers in a file. In this chapter, you will learn to define and pass regular expressions to grep, a command on Unix-like operating systems that searches a file for patterns and returns the text it finds in the file that matches the pattern. You will also learn to use regular expressions to search strings for patterns in Python.

Setup

To get started, create a file called zen.txt. From the command-line (make sure you are inside the directory where you created zen.txt) enter the command python3 -c "import this". This will print The Zen of Python, a poem by Tim Peters:

The Zen of Python
Beautiful is better than ugly.
Explicit is better than implicit.
Simple is better than complex.
Complex is better than complicated.
Flat is better than nested.
Sparse is better than dense.
Readability counts.
Special cases aren't special enough to break the rules.
Although practicality beats purity.
Errors should never pass silently.
Unless explicitly silenced.
In the face of ambiguity, refuse the temptation to guess.
There should be one—and preferably only one—obvious way to do it.
Although that way may not be obvious at first unless you're Dutch.
Now is better than never.
Although never is often better than *right* now.
If the implementation is hard to explain, it's a bad idea.
If the implementation is easy to explain, it may be a good idea.

Namespaces are one honking great idea—let's do more of those!

The -c flag tells Python you are going to pass it a string containing Python code. Python then executes the code. When Python executes import this, it prints The Zen of Python (a message hidden in code like this poem is called an **Easter egg**). Enter the function exit() into Bash to quit Python, then copy and paste The Zen of Python into the file zen.txt.

By default, on Ubuntu, the grep command prints matched words in red in its output, but on Unix it does not. If you are using a Mac, you can change this by setting the following environmental variables in Bash:

```
# http://tinyurl.com/z9prphe

$ export GREP_OPTIONS='--color=always'
```

Remember, setting an environmental variable in Bash is not permanent, so if you exit Bash you have to set the environmental variables again the next time you open it. You can add environmental variables to your .profile file to make them permanent.

A Simple Match

The grep command accepts two parameters: a regular expression and the filepath of the file to search for the pattern defined in the regular expression. The simplest kind of pattern to match with a regular expression is a simple match, a string of words that matches the same string of words. To see an example of a simple match, enter the following command in the directory where you created the file zen.txt:

```
# http://tinyurl.com/jgh3x4c

$ grep Beautiful zen.txt
```

```
>> Beautiful is better than ugly.
```

In the command you executed, the first parameter, Beautiful, is the regular expression, and the second parameter, zen.txt, is the path to the file to look for the regular expression in. Bash printed the line Beautiful is better than ugly. with Beautiful in **red** because it is the word the regular expression matched.

If you change the regular expression in the previous example from `Beautiful` to `beautiful`, `grep` will not match anything:

```
# http://tinyurl.com/j2z6t2r

$ grep beautiful zen.txt
```

You can ignore case with the flag `-i`:

```
# http://tinyurl.com/zchmrdq

$ grep -i beautiful zen.txt
```

>> **Beautiful** is better than ugly.

By default, `grep` prints the entire line (of the file) it found a match in. You can add the flag `-o` to only print the exact words that match the pattern you passed in:

```
# http://tinyurl.com/zfcdnmx

$ grep -o Beautiful zen.txt
```

>> **Beautiful**

You can use regular expressions in Python with its built-in library, `re` (regular expressions). The `re` module comes with a method called `findall`. You pass in a regular expression as a parameter, then a string and it returns a list with all the items in the string that the pattern matches:

```
1   # http://tinyurl.com/z9q2286
2
3
4   import re
5
6
7   l = "Beautiful is better than ugly."
8
9
10  matches = re.findall("Beautiful", l)
11
12
13  print(matches)
```

>> ['Beautiful']

In this example, the findall method found a match and returned a list with the match (Beautiful) as the first item.

You can ignore case in the findall method by passing in re.IGNORECASE to the findall method as the third parameter:

```
1   # http://tinyurl.com/jzeonne
2
3
4   import re
5
6
7   l = "Beautiful is better than ugly."
8
9
10  matches = re.findall("beautiful",
11                       l,
12                       re.IGNORECASE)
13
14
15  print(matches)
```

>> ['Beautiful']

Match Beginning and End

You can create regular expressions that match complex patterns by adding special characters to them that don't match a character but instead define a rule. For example, you can use the caret character (^) to create a regular expression that only matches a pattern if the pattern occurs at the beginning of a line:

```
# http://tinyurl.com/gleyzan

$ grep ^If zen.txt
```

```
>> If the implementation is hard to
explain, it's a bad idea.
>> If the implementation is easy to
explain, it may be a good idea.
```

Similarly, you can use the dollar sign ($) only to match the lines that end with a pattern:

```
# http://tinyurl.com/zkvpc2r

$ grep idea.$ zen.txt
```

```
>> If the implementation is hard to explain,
it's a bad idea.
>> If the implementation is easy to explain,
it may be a good idea.
```

In this case, grep ignored the line `Namespaces are one honking great idea -- let's do more of those!` because, although it contains the word `idea`, it does not end with it. Here is an example of using the caret symbol (^) in Python (you have to pass in `re.MULTILINE` as the third parameter to `indall` to look for matches on all of the lines of a multi-line string):

```
 1  # http://tinyurl.com/zntqzc9
 2
 3
 4  import re
 5
 6
 7  zen = """Although never is
 8  often better than
 9  *right* now.
10  If the implementation
11  is hard to explain,
12  it's a bad idea.
13  If the implementation
14  is easy to explain,
15  it may be a good
16  idea. Namespaces
17  are one honking
18  great idea -- let's
19  do more of those!
20  """
21
22
23  m = re.findall("^If",
24                    zen,
25                    re.MULTILINE)
26  print(m)
```

>> ['If', 'If']

Match Multiple Characters

You can define a pattern that matches multiple characters by putting them inside of brackets in a regular expression. If you put [abc] in a regular expression, it will match a, b, or c. In the next example, instead of matching text in your zen.txt file, you are going to look for a match in a string by piping it to grep:

```
# http://tinyurl.com/jf9qzuz

$ echo Two too. | grep -i t[ow]o
```

> **Two too**

The output of the command echo is passed to grep as input and, therefore, you don't need to specify the file parameter for grep. The command prints both two and too, because the regular expression matches a t, followed by an o or a w, followed by an o.

In Python:

```
1   # http://tinyurl.com/hg9sw3u
2
3
4   import re
5
6
7   string = "Two too."
8
9
10  m = re.findall("t[ow]o",
11                    string,
12                    re.IGNORECASE)
13  print(m)
```

>> ['Two', 'too']

Match Digits

You can match digits in a string with [[:digit:]]:

```
# http://tinyurl.com/gm8o6gb

$ echo 123 hi 34 hello. | grep [[:digit:]]
```

>> **123** hi **34** hello.

And \d in Python:

```
 1  # http://tinyurl.com/z3hr4q8
 2
 3
 4  import re
 5
 6
 7  line = "123?34 hello?"
 8
 9
10  m = re.findall("\d",
11                 line,
12                 re.IGNORECASE)
13
14
15  print(m)
```

>> ['1', '2', '3', '3', '4']

Repetition

The asterisk symbol (*) adds repetition to your regular expressions. With an asterisk, "the preceding item will be matched zero or more times."[12] For instance, you can use an asterisk to match tw followed by any amount of os:

```
# http://tinyurl.com/j8vbwq8

$ echo two twoo not too. | grep -o two*
```

>> two
>> twoo

In a regular expression, a period matches any character. If you follow a period with an asterisk, it instructs the regular expression to match any character zero or more times. You can use a period followed by an asterisk to match everything between two characters:

```
# http://tinyurl.com/h5x6cal

$ echo __hello__there | grep -o __.*__
```

>> __hello__

The regular expression __.*__ matches any character between and including the two double underscores. An asterisk is **greedy**, which means that it will try to match as much text as it can. For example, if you add more words with double underscores, the regular expression from the previous example will match everything from the first underscore to the last underscore:

```
# http://tinyurl.com/j9v9t24

$ echo __hi__bye__hi__there | grep -o __.*__
```

>> __hi__bye__hi__

You do not always want to match patterns greedily. You can follow an asterisk with a question mark to make the regular expression non-greedy. A **non-greedy** regular expression looks for the least number of matches possible. In this case, it would stop matching on the first double underscore it comes across, instead of matching everything between the very first underscore and the very last underscore. Grep does not have nongreedy matching, but in Python, you can use a question mark for non-greedy matching:

```
 1  # http://tinyurl.com/j399sq9
 2
 3
 4  import re
 5
 6
 7  t = "__one__ __two__ __three__"
 8
 9
10  found = re.findall("__.*?__", t)
11
12
13  for match in found:
14      print(match)
```

>> __one__
>> __two__
>> __three__

You can use non-greedy matching in Python to create the game Mad Libs (if you don't remember Mad Libs, it is a game with a paragraph of text with various words missing that the players are prompted to fill in):

```
1   # http://tinyurl.com/ze6oyua
2
3   import re
4
5
6   text = """Giraffes have aroused
7    the curiosity of __PLURAL_NOUN__
8    since earliest times. The
9    giraffe is the tallest of all
10   living __PLURAL_NOUN__, but
11   scientists are unable to
12   explain how it got its long
13   __PART_OF_THE_BODY__. The
14   giraffe's tremendous height,
15   which might reach __NUMBER__
16   __PLURAL_NOUN__, comes from
17   it legs and __BODYPART__.
18   """
19
20
21   def mad_libs(mls):
22       """
23       :param mls: String
24       with parts the user
25       should fill out surrounded
26       by double underscores.
27       Underscores cannot
28       be inside hint e.g., no
29       __hint_hint__ only
30       __hint__.
31       """
32       hints = re.findall("__.*?__",
33                           mls)
34       if hints is not None:
35           for word in hints:
36               q = "Enter a {}".format(word)
37               new = input(q)
38               mls = mls.replace(word, new, 1)
39           print('\n')
40           mls = mls.replace("\n", "")
41           print(mls)
```

```
42        else:
43            print("invalid mls")
44
45
46    mad_libs(text)
```

```
>> enter a __PLURAL_NOUN__
```

In this example, you use the `re.findall` method to get a list of all of the words in the variable `text` surrounded by double underscores (each one is a hint for the type of word the user needs to replace). Then, you loop through the list and use each hint to ask the person using the program to supply a new word. You then create a new string, replacing the hint with the user-supplied word. Once the loop finishes, you print the new string with all of the words you collected from the user.

Escaping

You can escape characters (ignore a character's meaning and match it instead) in regular expressions like you did earlier with strings in Python, by prefixing a character in a regular expression with a backslash \:

```
# http://tinyurl.com/zkbumfj

$ echo I love $ | grep \\$
```

```
>> I love $
```

Normally, the dollar sign means a match is only valid if it occurs at the end of the line, however, because you escaped it, your regular expression matches the dollar sign character instead.

And in Python:

```
 1  # http://tinyurl.com/zy7pr4l
 2
 3
 4  import re
 5
 6
 7  line = "I love $"
 8
 9
10  m = re.findall("\\\$",
11                 line,
12                 re.IGNORECASE)
13
14
15  print(m)
```

>> ['$']

Regular Expression Tool

Getting a regular expression to match a pattern is frustrating. Visit http://theselftaughtprogrammer.io/regex for a list of tools to help you create perfect regular expressions.

Vocabulary

Regular Expressions: A "sequence of characters that define a search pattern."[13]
Easter egg: A message hidden in code.
Greedy: A regular expression that is greedy will try to match text as it can.
Non-greedy: A non-greedy regular expression looks for the least number of matches possible.

Challenges

1. Write a regular expression that matches the word Dutch in The Zen of Python.
2. Come up with a regular expression that matches all the digits in the string Arizona 479, 501, 870. California 209, 213, 650.
3. Create a regular expression that matches any word that starts with any character and is followed by two o's. Then use Python's re module to match boo and loo in the sentence The ghost that says boo haunts the loo.

Solutions: http://tinyurl.com/jmlkvxm.

Chapter 18. Package Managers

"Every programmer is an author."
—Sercan Leylek

A **package manager** is a program that installs and manages other programs. They are useful because you often need to use other programs to create new software. For example, web developers often use a **web framework**: a program that helps you build a website. Programmers use package managers to install web frameworks, as well as a variety of other programs. In this chapter, you will learn to use the package manager **pip**.

Packages

A **package** is software "packaged" for distribution—it includes the files that make up the actual program, as well as **metadata**: data about data like the software's name, version number, and **dependencies**: the programs a program relies on to run properly. You can use a package manager to download a package and install it as a program on your computer. The package manager handles downloading any dependencies the package has.

Pip

In this section, I will show you how to use pip, a package manager for Python, to download Python packages. Once you've downloaded a package with pip, you can import it as a module in a Python program. First, check to see if pip is installed on your computer by opening Bash, or the Command Prompt if you are using Windows, and entering the command `pip3`:

```
# http://tinyurl.com/hmookdf


$ pip3
```

```
  > Usage: pip3 <command> [options] Commands:
install Install packages. download Download
packages. ...
```

When you enter the command, a list of options should print. Pip comes with Python when you download it, but it didn't in earlier versions. You will get a "command not found" error (or something similar, depending on your shell) if pip is not installed on your computer. Visit http://www.theselftaughtprogrammerio/pip for instructions on installing it.

You can install a new package with `pip3 install [package_name]`. Pip installs new packages into a folder in your Python directory called site-packages. You can find a list of all the Python packages available for download at https://pypi.python.org/pypi. There are two ways to specify the package you want to download—the package name, or the package name followed by two equal signs (==) and the version number you want to download. If you use the package name, pip will download the most recent version of the package. The second option allows you to download a particular package version, instead of the most current. Here is how to install `Flask`, a Python package for creating websites on Ubuntu and Unix:

```
# http://tinyurl.com/hchso7u

$ sudo pip3 install Flask==0.11.1
```

```
>> Password:
>> Successfully installed flask-0.11.1
```

On Windows, you need to use the command-line as an administrator. Right-click on the command-prompt icon and select `Run as administrator`.

Inside the Command Prompt enter:

```
# http://tinyurl.com/hyxm3vt

$ pip3 install Flask==0.11.1
```

```
>> Successfully installed flask-0.11.1
```

With this command, pip installs the `Flask` module in your computer's `site-packages` folder.

Now, you can import the `Flask` module in a program. Create a new Python file, add the following code, and run the program:

```
 1  # http://tinyurl.com/h59sdyu
 2
 3
 4  from flask import Flask
 5
 6
 7  app = Flask(__name__)
 8
 9
10  @app.route('/')
11  def index():
12      return "Hello, World!"
13
14
15  app.run(port='8000')
```

```
>> * Running on http://127.0.0.1:8000/ (Press CTRL+C to
quit)
```

Now, navigate to http://127.0.0.1:8000/ in your web browser, and you should see a website that says Hello, World!

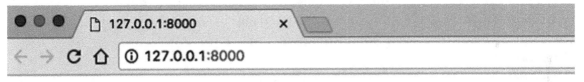

Hello, World!

The Flask module allows you to create a web server and a website quickly. Visit http://flask.pocoo.org/docs/0.11/tutorial to learn more about how this example works. You can view the packages you've installed with the command pip3 freeze:

```
# http://tinyurl.com/zxgcqeh

$ pip3 freeze
```

```
>> Flask==0.11.11
...
```

Finally, you can uninstall a program with `pip3 uninstall [package_name]`. Uninstall Flask with the following command:

```
# http://tinyurl.com/ht8mleo

$ pip3 uninstall flask
...
```

  >> Proceed (y/n)? y ...

Flask is now uninstalled, which you can verify with the command `pip3 freeze`.

Virtual Environments

Eventually, you will want to install your Python packages into a **virtual environment** instead of installing all of your packages into `site-packages`. Virtual environments allow you to keep the Python packages for your different programming projects separate. You can learn more about virtual environments at http://docs.python-guide.org/en/latest/dev/virtualenvs/.

Vocabulary

Package manager: A program that installs and manages other programs.
Web framework: A program that helps you build a website.
Package: Software "packaged" for distribution.
Metadata: Data about data.
Dependencies: The programs a program relies on to run properly.
Apt-get: A package manager that comes with Ubuntu.
Pip: A package manager for Python.
$PYTHONPATH: Python looks for modules in a list of folders stored in an environmental variable called `$PYTHONPATH`.
Site-packages: A folder in `$PYTHONPATH`. This folder is where pip installs packages.
PyPI: A website that hosts Python packages.
Virtual environment: You use a virtual environment to keep the Python packages for your different programming projects separate.

Challenge

1. Find a package on PyPI (https://pypi.python.org) and download it with pip.

Solution: http://tinyurl.com/h96qbw2.

Chapter 19. Version Control

"I object to doing things that computers can do."
—Olin Shivers

Writing software is a team sport. When you are working on a project with another person (or an entire team), you all need to be able to make changes to the **codebase**—the folders and files that make up your software, and you need to keep those changes in sync. You could periodically email each other with your changes and combine multiple different versions yourself, but that would be tedious.

Also, what would happen if you both made changes to the same part of the project? How do you decide whose changes to use? These are the kinds of problems a **version control system** solves. A version control system is a program designed to help you easily collaborate on projects with other programmers.

Git and **SVN** are two popular version control systems. Typically, you use a version control system in conjunction with a service that stores your software in the cloud. In this chapter, you will use Git to put software on **GitHub**, a website that stores your code on the cloud.

Repositories

A **repository** is a data structure created by a version control system, like Git, that keeps track of all the changes in your programming project. A **data structure** is a way of organizing and storing information: lists and dictionaries are examples of data structures (you will learn more about data structures in Part IV). When you see a repository, it will look like a directory with files in it. You will use Git to interact with the data structure that keeps track of the project's changes.

When you are working on a project managed by Git, there will be multiple repositories (usually one for each person working on the project). Typically, everybody working on the project has a repository on their computer called a **local repository**, which keeps track of all the changes they make to the project. There is also a **central repository**, hosted on a website like GitHub, that all the local repositories communicate with to stay in sync with each other (each repository is completely separate). A programmer working on the project can update the central repository with the changes they've made in their local repository, and they can update their local repository with the newest changes other programmers have made to the central repository. If you are working on a project with one other programmer, your setup will look like this:

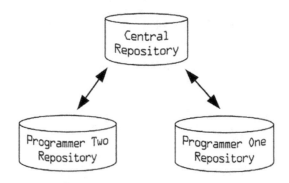

You can create a new central repository from GitHub's website (or the command-line). Once you create a central repository, you can use Git to create a local repository that communicates with it.

Getting Started

If GitHub changes the layout of their website, the instructions in this section will change. If that happens, I will provide new instructions at http://theselftaughtprogrammer.io/git. To get started, you need to create a GitHub account at https://github.com/join. To create a new repository on GitHub, login to your GitHub account (once you have created it) and click on the + button at the top right corner of the screen. Click New repository from the drop-down menu. Give the repository the name hangman. Select the Public option, and check the box Initialize the repository with a README. Now, click Create repository.

On GitHub, hit the button in the top right corner and select Your profile.

You will see the name of your repository: `hangman`. Click on it. This part of the website is your central repository. You will see a button that says `Clone Or Download`. When you click on it, you will see a link. Save this link.

Before you can precede, you need to install Git. You can find installation instructions at https://www.git-scm.com/book/en/v2/Getting-Started-Installing-Git.

Once you have installed Git, you can use it from the command-line. Type `git` into the command-line:

```
# http://tinyurl.com/gs9d5hf
$ git
```

```
>> usage: git [--version] [--help] [-C <path>] [-c
name=value] ...
```

If your output looks like this example, you've correctly installed Git.

Now you can use the link you found earlier to download a local repository to your computer with the command `git clone [repository_url]`. The repository will download in whatever directory you issue the command from. Copy the link, or press the copy link to clipboard button, and pass it to the `git clone` command:

```
# http://tinyurl.com/hvmq98m

$ git clone [repository_url]
```

```
>> Cloning into 'hangman'... remote: Counting objects:
3, done. remote: Total 3 (delta 0), reused 0 (delta 0),
packreused 0 Unpacking objects: 100% (3/3), done. Checking
connectivity... done.
```

Use `ls` to verify the local repository downloaded:

```
# http://tinyurl.com/gp4o9qv

$ ls
>> hangman
```

You should see a directory called `hangman`. This directory is your local repository.

Pushing and Pulling

There are two main things you can do with Git. The first is updating your central repository with changes from your local repository, called **pushing**. The second is updating your local repository with new changes from your central repository, called **pulling**.

The command git remote -v (a common flag that usually prints extra information and stands for verbose) prints the URL of the central repository your local repository is pushing to and pulling from. Enter your hangman directory and use the git remote command:

```
# http://tinyurl.com/jscq6pj

$ cd hangman
$ git remote -v
```

```
>> origin [your_url]/hangman.git (fetch)
>> origin [your_url]/hangman.git (push)
```

The first line of output is the URL for the central repository your project will pull data from, and the second line is the URL for the central repository your project will push data to. Typically, you will push to and pull from the same central repository so that the URLs will be the same.

Pushing Example

In this section, you are going to make a change to the local hangman repository you created and cloned to your computer, then push that change to your central repository hosted on GitHub.

Move your Python file into the hangman directory with the code from the challenge you completed at the end of Part I. Your local repository now has a file that does not exist in your central repository—it is out of sync with your central repository. You can resolve this by pushing the change you made in your local repository to your central repository.

You push changes from your local repository to your central repository in three steps. First, you **stage** your files: you tell Git which modified files you want to push to your central repository.

The command git status shows the current state of your project in relation to your repository, so you can decide what files to stage. The git status command prints the files in your local repository that differ from your central repository. When you unstage a file it is in red. When you stage a file, it is in green. Make sure you are in your hangman directory and enter the command git status:

```
# http://tinyurl.com/jvcr59w

$ git status
```

>> On branch master Your branch is up-to-date with 'origin/master'. Untracked files: (use "git add <file>..." to include in what will be committed)

hangman.py

You should see the file hangman.py in **red**. You can stage a file with the command git add [file]:

```
# http://tinyurl.com/hncnyz9

$ git add hangman.py
```

Now use the command git status to confirm you staged the file:

```
# http://tinyurl.com/jeuug7j

$ git status
```

>> On branch master Your branch is up-to-date with 'origin/
master'. Changes to be committed: (use "git reset HEAD
<file>..." to unstage)

new file: hangman.py

The file `hangman.py` is *green* because you staged it.

You can unstage a file without making changes to your central repository with the syntax `git reset [file_path]`. Unstage `hangman.py` with:

```
# http://tinyurl.com/hh6xxvw

$ git reset hangman.py.
```

Confirm it was unstaged with `git status`:

>> On branch master Your branch is up-to-date with 'origin/
master'. Untracked files: (use "git add <file>..." to include
in what will be committed)

hangman.py

Stage it again:

```
# http://tinyurl.com/gowe7hp

$ git add hangman.py
$ git status
```

>> On branch master Your branch is up-to-date with 'origin/
master'. Changes to be committed: (use "git reset HEAD
<file>..." to unstage)

new file: hangman.py

Once you've staged the files you want to update your central repository with, you are ready to move to the next step, **committing** your files—giving a command to Git to record the changes you made in your local repository. You can commit your files with the syntax `git commit -m [your_message]`. This command creates a **commit**: a version of your project that Git saves. The `-m` flag means you are going to add a message to your commit to help you remember what changes you are making and why (this message is like a comment). In the next step, you are going to push your changes to your central repository on GitHub, where you will be able to view your message:

```
# http://tinyurl.com/gmn92p6

$ git commit -m "my first commit"
```

>> 1 file changed, 1 insertion(+) create mode 100644 hangman.py

Once you've committed your files, you are ready for the final step. You can now push your changes to your central repository with the command `git push origin master`:

```
# http://tinyurl.com/hy98yq9

$ git push origin master
```

>> 1 file changed, 1 insertion(+) create mode 100644 hangman.py Corys-MacBook-Pro:hangman coryalthoff$ git push origin master Counting objects: 3, done. Delta compression using up to 4 threads. Compressing objects: 100% (2/2), done. Writing objects: 100% (3/3), 306 bytes | 0 bytes/s, done. Total 3 (delta 0), reused 0 (delta 0) To https:// github.com/coryalthoff/hangman.git f5d44da..b0dab51 master -> master

After you enter your username and password into the command-line, the `git` program will push your changes to GitHub. If you look at your central repository on GitHub's website, you will see `hangman.py`, as well as the message you made in your commit.

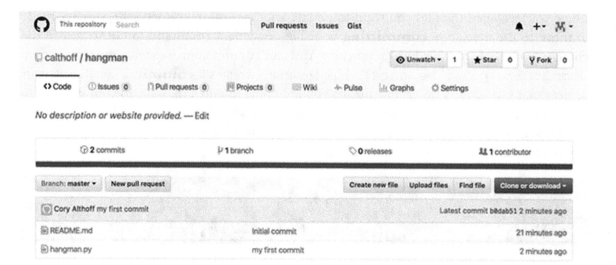

Pulling Example

In this section, you are going to update your local repository by pulling the changes from your central repository. You will need to do this whenever you want to update your local repository with the changes another programmer made to the central repository.

Go to your central repository and press the button `Create new file`. Create a file called `new.py` and then press the button `Commit new file`. This file is not yet in your local repository, so your local repository is out of sync with your central repository. You can update your local repository with changes from your central repository with the command `git pull origin master`:

```
# http://tinyurl.com/gqf2xue

$ git pull origin master
```

```
>> remote: Counting objects: 3, done. remote: Compressing
objects: 100% (2/2), done. remote: Total 3 (delta 0),
reused 0 (delta 0), pack-reused 0 Unpacking objects: 100%
(3/3), done. From https://github.com/coryalthoff/hangman
b0dab51..8e032f5 master -> origin/master Updating
b0dab51..8e032f5 Fast-forward new.py | 1 + 1 file changed,
1 insertion(+) create mode 100644 new.py
```

Git applied the changes from your central repository to your local repository. The `new.py` file you created in your central repository should now be in your local repository. Confirm with `ls`:

```
$ ls
```

```
>> README.md hangman.py new.py
```

Reverting Versions

Git saves your project every time you commit a file. With Git, you can revert to any previous commit—you can "rewind" your project. For example, you can return your project back to a commit you made last week. All of your files and folders will be the same as they were last week. Then you can immediately jump forward to a more recent commit. Each commit has a **commit number**: a unique sequence of characters that Git uses to identify a commit.

You can view your project's history of commits with the command `git log`, which prints all of your commits:

```
# http://tinyurl.com/h2m7ahs

$ git log
```

```
>> commit 8e032f54d383e5b7fc640a3686067ca14fa8b43f Author:
Cory Althoff <coryedwardalthoff@gmail.com> Date: Thu Dec 8
16:20:03 2016 -0800

Create new.py
commit b0dab51849965144d78de21002464dc0f9297fdc Author:
Cory Althoff <coryalthoff@Corys-MacBook-Pro.local> Date:
Thu Dec 8 16:12:10 2016 -0800

my first commit
commit f5d44dab1418191f6c2bbfd4a2b2fcf74ef5a68f Author:
Cory Althoff <coryedwardalthoff@gmail.com> Date: Thu Dec 8
15:53:25 2016 -0800 Initial commit
```

You should see three commits. Your first commit was when you created the central repository. Your second commit was when you updated the central repository with your `hangman.py` file. Your third commit was when you created the file `new.py`. Each commit has a commit number. You can switch your project to another commit by passing a commit number to the command `git checkout`. In this example, I could revert my project to what it looked like when I first created it with the command `git checkout f5d44dab1418191f6c2bbfd4a2b2fcf74ef5a68f`.

diff

The command `git diff` shows you the difference between a file in your local repository versus your central repository. Create a new file called `hello_world.py` in your local repository, and add the code `print("Hello, World!")` to it.

Now stage the file:

```
# http://tinyurl.com/h6msygd

$ git add hello_world.py
```

Make sure everything looks right:

```
# http://tinyurl.com/zg4d8vd

$ git status
```

>> Changes to be committed: (use "git reset HEAD <file>..." to unstage) *new file: hello_world.py*

And commit it:

```
# http://tinyurl.com/ztcm8zs

$ git commit -m "adding new file"
```

>> 1 file changed, 1 insertion(+) create mode 100644 hello_world.py

Push your changes to your central repository:

```
# http://tinyurl.com/zay2vct

$ git push origin master
```

>> Counting objects: 3, done. Delta compression using
up to 4 threads. Compressing objects: 100% (2/2), done.
Writing objects: 100% (3/3), 383 bytes | 0 bytes/s, done.
Total 3 (delta 0), reused 0 (delta 0) To https://github.
com/coryalthoff/hangman.git 8e032f5..6f679b1 master ->
master

Now add print("Hello!") to the second line of the hello_world.py file in your local repository. Now, that file is different from the file in your central repository. Enter the command git diff to see the difference:

```
# http://tinyurl.com/znvj9r8

$ git diff hello_world.py
```

>> diff --git a/hello_world.py b/hello_world.py index
b376c99..83f9007 100644 --- a/hello_world.py +++
b/hello_world.py -1 +1,2 print("Print, Hello World!")
+print("Hello!")

Git highlights print("Hello!") in *green* because it is a new line of code. The addition (+) operator means this line is new. If you had removed code, the deleted code would be in red and preceded by a subtraction operator (-).

Next Steps

In this chapter, I covered the features of Git you will use most frequently. Once you've mastered the basics, I recommend you spend time learning about Git's more advanced features like branching and merging at http://theselftaughtprogrammer.io/git.

Vocabulary

Codebase: The folders and files that make up your software.
Version control system: A program designed to let you easily collaborate on projects with other programmers.

Git: A popular version control system.

SVN: A popular version control system.

GitHub: A website that stores your code on the cloud.

Repository: A data structure created by a version control system, like Git, that keeps track of the changes in your programming project.

Data structure: A way of organizing and storing information. Lists and dictionaries are examples of data structures.

Local repository: The repository on your computer.

Central repository: A repository hosted on a website like GitHub that all of the local repositories communicate with to stay in sync with each other.

Pushing: Updating your central repository with changes from your local repository.

Pulling: Updating your local repository with changes from your central repository.

Staging: Telling Git which files (with modifications) you want to push to your central repository.

Committing: Giving a command that tells Git to record the changes you made in your repository.

Commit: A version of your project that Git saves.

Commit number: A unique sequence of characters Git uses to identify a commit.

Challenges

1. Create a new repository on GitHub. Put all your Python files from the exercises you've completed so far into one directory on your computer and push them to your new repository.

Chapter 20. Bringing It All Together

"The magic of myth and legend has come true in our time. One types the correct incantation on a keyboard, and a display screen comes to life, showing things that never were nor could be..."
—Frederick Brooks

In this chapter, you will see how powerful programming is by building a **web scraper**: a program that extracts data from a website. Once you can build a web scraper, you have the ability to collect data from the largest collection of information in existence. The power of web scrapers, and how easy they are to build, is one of the reasons I got hooked on programming, and I hope it has the same effect on you.

HTML

Before you build a web scraper, you need a quick primer on **HTML**: hypertext markup language. HTML is one of the fundamental technologies programmers build websites with, along with CSS and JavaScript. HTML is a language that gives a website structure. HTML is made up of tags a web browser uses to layout web pages. You can build an entire website with HTML. It won't be interactive or look very good, because JavaScript is what makes websites interactive, and CSS is what gives them style, but it will be a website. Here is a website that displays the text Hello, World!

```
# http://tinyurl.com/jptzkvp


<!--This is a comment in HTML.
Save this file as index.html-->
<!-- http://tinyurl.com/h3bjuov -->


<html lang="en">
<head>
    <meta charset="UTF-8">
    <title>My Website</title>
</head>
<body>
    Hello, World!
    <a href="https://www.google.com"/>
    here</a>
</body>
</html>
```

Save this HTML into a file. Open the file with your web browser by clicking on the file (you may have to right-click and change the default program to open the file with a web browser like Chrome). Once you've opened the file with your web browser, you will see a website that says Hello World! with a link to Google.

Hello, World! here

Your web browser uses the different **HTML tags** in your HTML file to display this website. An HTML tag (tag for short) is like a programming keyword—it tells your browser to do something. Most tags have a beginning tag and closing tag, often with text in between. For example, your browser displays the text in between the <title> </title> tags in the tab of your browser. You can have tags within tags; everything in between <head></head> is metadata about the web page, whereas everything in between <body></body> makes up the actual site. Together, the <a></a> tags create a link. Tags can hold data. For example, href="https://www.google.com" inside of the <a> tag lets the browser know what website to link to. There is a lot more to HTML, but with this knowledge you are ready to build your first web scraper.

Scrape Google News

In this section, you are going to build a web scraper that fetches all of the stories from Google News by extracting all the <a></a> tags from Google News' HTML. Google News uses these tags to link to the different websites that make up the site, so in addition to some extra data, you will collect all the URLs for the stories Google News is displaying. You will use the BeautifulSoup module to **parse** Google News' HTML. Parsing means taking a format like HTML and using a programming language to give it structure. For example, turning the data into an object. To get started, use the follow command to install the BeautifulSoup module on Ubuntu and Unix:

```
# http://tinyurl.com/z4fzfzf

$ sudo pip3 install beautifulsoup4==4.4.1
```

>> Successfully installed beautifulsoup4-4.4.1

And on Windows (open the command-line as administrator):

```
# http://tinyurl.com/hk3kxgr


$ pip3 install beautifulsoup4==4.4.1
```

>> Successfully installed beautifulsoup4-4.4.1

Python has a built-in module, named urllib, for working with URLs. Add the following code to a new Python file:

```
1   # http://tinyurl.com/jmgyar8
2
3
4   import urllib.request
5   from bs4 import BeautifulSoup
6
7
8   class Scraper:
9       def __init__(self,
10                       site):
11          self.site = site
12
13
14      def scrape(self):
15          pass
```

The __init__ method takes a website to scrape from as a parameter. Later, you will pass in "https://news.google.com/" as a parameter. The Scraper class has a method called scrape you will call whenever you want to scrape data from the site you passed in.

Add the following code to your scrape method:

```
1   # http://tinyurl.com/h5eywoa
2
3
4   def scrape(self):
5       r = urllib.request.urlopen(self.site)
6       html = r.read()
```

The urlopen() function makes a request to a website and returns a Response object that has its HTML stored in it, along with additional data. The function response.read() returns the HTML from the Response object. All of the HTML from the website is in the variable html.

Now you are ready to parse the HTML. Add a new line of code in the scrape function that creates a BeautifulSoup object, and pass in the html variable and the string "html.parser" (because you are parsing HTML) as a parameter:

```
1  # http://tinyurl.com/hvjulxh
2
3
4  def scrape(self):
5      r = urllib.request.urlopen(self.site)
6      html = r.read()
7      parser = "html.parser"
8      sp = BeautifulSoup(html, parser)
```

The BeautifulSoup object does all the hard work and parses the HTML. Now you can add code to the scrape function that calls the method find_all on the BeautifulSoup object. Pass in "a" as a parameter (which tells the function to look for <a></a> tags) and the method will return all of the URLs the website links to in the HTML you downloaded:

```
1   # http://tinyurl.com/zwrxjjk
2
3
4   def scrape(self):
5       r = urllib.request.urlopen(self.site)
6       html = r.read()
7       parser = "html.parser"
8       sp = BeautifulSoup(html, parser)
9       for tag in sp.find_all("a"):
10          url = tag.get("href")
11          if url is None:
12              continue
13          if "html" in url:
14              print("\n" + url)
```

The find_all method returns an iterable containing the tag objects it found. Each time around the for-loop, the variable tag is assigned the value of a new Tag object. Each Tag object has many different instance variables, but you just want the value of the href instance variable, which contains each URL. You can get it by calling the method get and passing in "href" as a parameter. Finally, you check that the variable URL contains data; that it has the string "html" in it (you don't want to print internal links); and if it does, you print it. Here is the complete web scraper:

```
1   # http://tinyurl.com/j55s7hm
2
3
4   import urllib.request
5   from bs4 import BeautifulSoup
6
7
8   class Scraper:
9       def __init__(self, site):
10          self.site = site
11
12
13      def scrape(self):
14          r = urllib.request.urlopen(self.site)
15          html = r.read()
16          parser = "html.parser"
17          sp = BeautifulSoup(html, parser)
18          for tag in sp.find_all("a"):
19              url = tag.get("href")
20              if url is None:
21                  continue
22              if "html" in url:
23                  print("\n" + url)
24
25
26  news = "https://news.google.com/"
27  Scraper(news).scrape()
```

When you run your program, the output should look similar to this:

https://www.washingtonpost.com/world/national-security/in-foreign-bribery-cases-leniency-offered-to-companies-that-turn-over-employees/2016/04/05/d7a24d94-fb43-11e5-9140-e61d062438bb_story.html?utm_term=.aab581385443

http://www.appeal-democrat.com/news/unit-apartment-complex-proposed-in-marysville/article_bd6ea9f2-fac3-11e5-bfaf-4fbe11089e5a.html

http://www.appeal-democrat.com/news/injuries-from-yuba-city-bar-violence-hospitalize-groom-to-be/article_03e46648-f54b-11e5-96b3-5bf32bfbf2b5.html

Now that you can collect Google News' headlines, the possibilities are limitless. You could write a program to analyze the most used words in the headlines. You could build a program to analyze the sentiment of the headlines, and see if it has any correlation with the stock market. With web scraping, all the information in the world is yours for the taking, and I hope that excites you as much as it does me.

Vocabulary

Web scraper: A program that extracts data from a website.
HTML: A language that gives a website structure.
HTML Tag: Like a programming keyword—it tells your browser to do something.
Parse: Parsing means taking a format like HTML and using a programming language to give it structure. For example, turning the data into an object.

Challenge

1. Modify your scraper to save the headlines in a file.

Challenge solution: http://tinyurl.com/gkv6fuh.

Part IV
Introduction to Computer Science

Chapter 21. Data Structures

"I will, in fact, claim that the difference between a bad programmer and a good one is whether he considers his code or his data structures more important. Bad programmers worry about the code. Good programmers worry about data structures and their relationships."
—Linus Torvalds

Data Structures

A **data structure** is a format used to store and organize information. Data structures are fundamental to programming, and most programming languages come with them built-in. You already know how to use several of Python's built-in data structures, such as lists, tuples, and dictionaries. In this chapter, you will learn how to create two more data structures: stacks and queues.

Stacks

A **stack** is a data structure. Like a list, you can add and remove items from a stack, except unlike a list, you can only add and remove the last item. If you have the list [1, 2, 3], you can remove any of the items in it. If you have a stack that is the same, you can only remove the last item in it, 3. If you remove the 3, your stack looks like [1, 2]. Now you can remove the 2. Once you've removed the 2, you can remove the 1, and the stack is empty. Removing an item from a stack is called **popping**. If you put 1 back on the stack, it looks like [1]. If you put a two onto the stack, it looks like [1, 2]. Putting an item onto a stack is called **pushing**. This kind of data structure, where the last item put in is the first item taken out, is called a **last-in-first-out data structure (LIFO)**.

You can think of a LIFO like a stack of dishes. If you stack five dishes on top of each other, you would have to remove all the other dishes to get to the one on the bottom of the stack. Think of every piece of data in a stack like a dish, to access it you have to pull out the data at the top.

In this section, you are going to build a stack. Python has a library with both of the data structures I cover in this chapter, but building your own will show you how they work. The stack will have five methods: is_empty, push, pop, and size. The method is_empty returns True if your stack is empty and False otherwise. push adds an item to the top of your stack. pop removes and returns the top item from your stack. peek returns the top item in the stack, but does not remove it. size returns an integer representing the number of items in your stack. Here is a stack implemented in Python:

```
1   # http://tinyurl.com/zk24ps6
2
3
4   class Stack:
5       def __init__(self):
6           self.items = []
7
8
9       def is_empty(self):
10          return self.items == []
11
12
13      def push(self, item):
14          self.items.append(item)
15
16
17      def pop(self):
18          return self.items.pop()
19
20
21      def peek(self):
22          last = len(self.items)-1
23          return self.items[last]
24
25
26      def size(self):
27          return len(self.items)
```

If you create a new stack, it will be empty, and the is_empty method will return True:

```
1   # http://tinyurl.com/jfybm4v
2
3
4   stack = Stack()
5   print(stack.is_empty())
```

>> True

When you add a new item to the stack, is_empty returns False:

```
1  # http://tinyurl.com/zsexcal
2
3
4  stack = Stack()
5  stack.push(1)
6  print(stack.is_empty())
```

>> False

Call the pop method to remove an item from the stack, and is_empty once again returns True:

```
1  # http://tinyurl.com/j72kswr
2
3
4  stack = Stack()
5  stack.push(1)
6  item = stack.pop()
7  print(item)
8  print(stack.is_empty())
```

>> 1
>> True

Finally, you can take a peek at a stack's contents and get its size:

```
1  # http://tinyurl.com/zle7sno
2
3
4  stack = Stack()
5
6
7  for i in range(0, 6):
8      stack.push(i)
9
10
11  print(stack.peek())
12  print(stack.size())
```

>> 5
>> 6

Reversing a String with a Stack

A stack can reverse an iterable, because whatever you put on a stack comes off in reverse order. In this section, you will solve a common programming interview problem—reversing a string using a stack by first putting it in on a stack, then taking it off:

```
1   # http://tinyurl.com/zoosvqg
2
3
4   class Stack:
5       def __init__(self):
6           self.items = []
7
8
9       def is_empty(self):
10          return self.items == []
11
12
13      def push(self, item):
14          self.items.append(item)
15
16
17      def pop(self):
18          return self.items.pop()
19
20
21      def peek(self):
22          last = len(self.items)-1
23          return self.items[last]
24
25
26      def size(self):
27          return len(self.items)
28
29
30  stack = Stack()
31  for c in "Hello":
32      stack.push(c)
33
```

```
34
35   reverse = ""
36
37
38   for i in range(len(stack.items)):
39       reverse += stack.pop()
40
41
42   print(reverse)
```

>> olleH

First, you went through each character in the string `"Hello"`, and put it in a stack. Then you iterated through the stack. You took each item off the stack and into the variable `reverse`. Once the iteration is complete, the original word is in reverse, and your program prints `olleH`.

Queues

A **queue** is another data structure. A queue is also like a list; you can add and remove items from it. A queue is also like a stack because you can only add and remove items in a certain order. Unlike a stack, where the first item put in is the last out, a queue is a **firstin- first-out data structure (FIFO)**: the first item added is the first item taken out.

Think of a FIFO data structure as a line of people waiting to buy movie tickets. The first person in line is the first person to get tickets, the second person in line is the second person to get tickets, and so on.

In this section, you will build a queue with four methods: `enqueue`, `dequeue`, `is_ empty`, and `size`. `enqueue` adds a new item to the queue; `dequeue` removes an item from the queue; `is_empty` returns `True` if the queue is empty and `False` otherwise; and `size` returns the number of items in the queue:

```
1   # http://tinyurl.com/zrg24hj
2
3
4   class Queue:
5       def __init__(self):
6           self.items = []
7
8
9       def is_empty(self):
10          return self.items == []
11
12
13      def enqueue(self, item):
14          self.items.insert(0, item)
15
16
17      def dequeue(self):
18          return self.items.pop()
19
20
21      def size(self):
22          return len(self.items)
```

If you create a new, empty queue, the is_empty method returns True:

```
1   # http://tinyurl.com/j3ck9jl
2
3
4   a_queue = Queue()
5   print(a_queue.is_empty())
```

>> True

Add items and check the queue's size:

```
1   # http://tinyurl.com/jzjrg8s
2
3
4   a_queue = Queue()
5
6
7   for i in range(5):
8       a_queue.enqueue(i)
9
10
11  print(a_queue.size())
```

>> 5

Remove each item from the queue:

```
1   # http://tinyurl.com/jazkh8b
2
3
4   a_queue = Queue()
5
6
7   for i in range(5):
8       a_queue.enqueue(i)
9
10
11  for i in range(5):
12      print(a_queue.dequeue())
13
14
15  print()
16
17
18  print(a_queue.size())
```

>> 0
>> 1
>> 2
>> 3
>> 4
>>
>> 0

Ticket Queue

A queue can simulate people waiting in line to buy tickets for a movie:

```
1   # http://tinyurl.com/jnw56zx
2
3
4   import time
5   import random
6
7
8   class Queue:
9       def __init__(self):
10          self.items = []
11
12
13      def is_empty(self):
14          return self.items == []
15
16
17      def enqueue(self, item):
18          self.items.insert(0, item)
19
20
21      def dequeue(self):
22          return self.items.pop()
23
24
25      def size(self):
26          return len(self.items)
27
28
29      def simulate_line(self, till_show, max_time):
30          pq = Queue()
31          tix_sold = []
32
33
34          for i in range(100):
35              pq.enqueue("person" + str(i))
36
```

```
37
38                    t_end = time.time() + till_show
39                    now = time.time()
40                    while now < t_end and not pq.is_empty():
41                        now = time.time()
42                        r = random.randint(0, max_time)
43                        time.sleep(r)
44                        person = pq.dequeue()
45                        print(person)
46                        tix_sold.append(person)
47
48
49                    return tix_sold
50
51
52    queue = Queue()
53    sold = queue.simulate_line(5, 1)
54    print(sold)

>> person0
...
>> ['person0', 'person1', 'person2']
```

First, you created a function called `simulate_line`, which simulates selling tickets to a line of people. The function accepts two parameters: `till_show` and `max_time`. The first parameter is an integer, representing the number of seconds until the show starts and there is no time left to buy tickets. The second parameter is also an integer, representing the longest amount of time (in seconds) it takes for a person to buy a ticket.

In the function, you create a new, empty queue and an empty list. The list will keep track of the people who purchased a ticket. Next, you fill the queue with one hundred strings, starting with `"person0"` and ending with `"person99"`. Each string in the queue represents a person in line waiting to buy a ticket.

The built-in `time` module has a function called `time`. It returns a float that represents the number of seconds it has been since the **epoch**, a point in time (January 1st, 1970) used as a reference. If I call the `time` function right now, it returns `1481849664.256039`, the number of seconds since the epoch. If in one second I call it again, the float the function returns will be incremented by 1.

The variable t_end finds the result of the time function plus the number of seconds passed in as the variable till_show. The combination of the two creates a point in the future.

Your while-loop runs until either the time function returns a result greater than t_end, or the queue is empty.

Next, you stop Python for a random amount of time to simulate that each ticket sale takes a different amount of time. You do this by calling the sleep function in the built-in time module to stop Python from doing anything for a random number of seconds between 0 and max_time.

After the pause caused by the sleep function, you remove a string representing a person from the queue and place it into the tix_sold list, which represents that the person bought a ticket.

The result of your code is a function that can sell tickets to a line of people, selling more or fewer tickets depending on the parameters passed in and random chance.

Vocabulary

Data structure: A format used to store and organize information.
Popping: Removing an item from a stack.
Pushing: Putting an item onto a stack.
Last-in- irst-out data structure: A data structure where the last item put in is the first item taken out.
LIFO: Last-in-first-out
Stack: A last-in-first-out data structure data structure.
First-in- irst-out data structure: A data structure where the first item added is the first item taken out.
FIFO: First-in-first-out Queue: A first-in-first-out data structure.
Epoch: A point in time used as a reference.

Challenges

1. Reverse the string "yesterday" using a stack.
2. Use a stack to create a new list with the items in the following list reversed: [1, 2, 3, 4, 5].

Solutions: http://tinyurl.com/j7d7nx2.

Chapter 22. Algorithms

"An algorithm is like a recipe."
—Waseem Latif

This chapter is a light introduction to algorithms. An **algorithm** is a series of steps that can be followed to solve a problem. The problem could be searching a list or printing the lyrics to "99 Bottles of Beer on the Wall."

FizzBuzz

It's finally time to learn to solve FizzBuzz, the popular interview question designed to eliminate candidates: Write a program that prints the numbers from 1 to 100. But for multiples of three print "Fizz" instead of the number, and for the multiples of five print "Buzz." For multiples of both three and five print "FizzBuzz."

To solve this problem, you need a way to check if a number is a multiple of three, a multiple of five, both, or neither. If a number is a multiple of three, if you divide it by three, there is no remainder. The same applies to five. The modulo operator (%) returns the remainder. You can solve this problem by iterating through the numbers and checking if each number is divisible by both three and five, just three, just five, or neither:

```
1   # http://tinyurl.com/jroprmn
2
3
4   def fizz_buzz():
5       for i in range(1, 101):
6           if i % 3 == 0 and i % 5 == 0:
7               print("FizzBuzz")
8           elif i % 3 == 0:
9               print("Fizz")
10          elif i % 5 == 0:
11              print("Buzz")
12          else:
13              print(i)
14
15
16  fizz_buzz()
```

```
>> 1
>> 2
>> Fizz
...
```

You start by iterating through numbers 1 to 100. Then, you check if the number is divisible by 3 and 5. It is important to do this first, because if a number is divisible by both, you need to print `FizzBuzz` and continue to the next iteration of the loop. If you checked if a number was divisible by just 3 or 5 first, and found a number that was, you cannot print `Fizz` or `Buzz` and continue to the next iteration of the loop, because the number could still be divisible by 3 and 5, in which case printing `Fizz` or `Buzz` is incorrect; you need to print `FizzBuzz`.

Once you've checked if a number is divisible by 3 and 5, the order of these two tests is no longer important, because you know it is not divisible by both. If the number is divisible by 3 or 5, you can stop the algorithm and print `Fizz` or `Buzz`. If a number makes it past the first three conditions, you know it is not divisible by 3, 5, or both, and you can print the number.

Sequential Search

A **search algorithm** finds information in a data structure like a list. A **sequential search** is a simple search algorithm that checks each item in a data structure to see if the item matches what it is looking for.

If you were ever playing cards and looking for a specific card in the deck, you probably did a sequential search to find it. You went through each card in the deck one by one, and if the card was not the one you were looking for, you moved on to the next card. When you finally came to the card you wanted, you stopped. If you made it through the entire deck without finding the card, you also stopped, because you realized the card wasn't there. Here is an example of a sequential search in Python:

```
1   # http://tinyurl.com/zer9esp
2
3
4   def ss(number_list, n):
5       found = False
6       for i in number_list:
7           if i == n:
8               found = True
9               break
10      return found
11
12
13  numbers = range(0, 100)
14  s1 = ss(numbers, 2)
15  print(s1)
16  s2 = ss(numbers, 202)
17  print(s2)
```

```
>> True
>> False
```

First, you set the variable found to False. This variable keeps track of whether or not the algorithm has found the number you are looking for. Then, you loop through every number in the list and check if it is that number. If it is, you set found to True, exit the loop, and return the variable found, which is True.

If you do not find the number you are looking for, you continue to the next number in the list. If you get through the entire list, you return the variable found. found will be False if the number isn't in the list.

Palindrome

A **palindrome** is a word spelled the same way forward and backward. You can write an algorithm that checks if a word is a palindrome by reversing all the letters in the word and testing if the reversed word and the original word are the same. If they are, the word is a palindrome:

```
 1  # http://tinyurl.com/jffr7pr
 2
 3
 4  def palindrome(word):
 5      word = word.lower()
 6      return word[::-1] == word
 7
 8
 9  print(palindrome("Mother"))
10  print(palindrome("Mom"))
```

```
>> False
>> True
```

The `lower` method removes uppercase characters from the word you are testing. Python treats M and m as different characters, and you want them treated as the same character.

The code `word[::-1]` reverses the word. `[::-1]` is Python's syntax for returning a slice of an entire iterable in reverse. You reverse the word so you can compare it to the original. If they are the same, the function returns `True`, because the word is a palindrome. If not, it returns `False`.

Anagram

An **anagram** is a word created by rearranging the letters of another word. The word iceman is an anagram of cinema, because you can rearrange the letters in either word to form the other. You can determine if two words are anagrams by sorting the letters in each word alphabetically and testing if they are the same:

```
 1  # http://tinyurl.com/hxplj3z
 2
 3
 4  def anagram(w1, w2):
 5      w1 = w1.lower()
 6      w2 = w2.lower()
 7      return sorted(w1) == sorted(w2)
 8
 9
10  print(anagram("iceman", "cinema"))
11  print(anagram("leaf", "tree"))
```

```
>> True
>> False
```

First, you call the `lower` method on both words so that case does not affect the result. Then, you pass both words into Python's `sorted` method. The `sorted` method returns the words sorted in alphabetical order. Finally, you compare the results. If the sorted words are the same, your algorithm returns `True`. Otherwise it returns `False`.

Count Character Occurrences

In this section, you are going to write an algorithm that returns the number of times each character occurs in a string. The algorithm will iterate character by character through the string, and keep track of how many times each character occurs in a dictionary:

```
1   # http://tinyurl.com/zknqlde
2
3
4   def count_characters(string):
5       count_dict = {}
6       for c in string:
7           if c in count_dict:
8               count_dict[c] += 1
9           else:
10              count_dict[c] = 1
11      print(count_dict)
12
13
14  count_characters("Dynasty")
```

```
>> {'D': 1, 't': 1, 'n': 1, 'a': 1, 's': 1, 'y': 2}
```

In this algorithm, you iterate through each character in a string passed in as the parameter `string`. If the character is already in the dictionary `count_dict`, you increment the value of the character by 1.

Otherwise, you add the character to the dictionary and set its value to 1. By the end of the for-loop, `count_dict` contains a key-value pair for each character in the string. The value of each key is the number of times it occurred in the string.

Recursion

Recursion is a method of solving problems by breaking the problem up into smaller and smaller pieces until it can be easily solved. So far, you've solved problems using **iterative algorithms**. Iterative algorithms solve problems by repeating steps over and over, typically using a loop. **Recursive algorithms** rely on functions that call themselves. Any problem you can solve iteratively can be solved recursively; however, sometimes a recursive algorithm is a more elegant solution.

You write a recursive algorithm inside of a function. The function must have a **base case**: a condition that ends a recursive algorithm to stop it from continuing forever. Inside the function, the function calls itself. Each time the function calls itself, it moves closer to the base case. Eventually, the base case condition is satisfied, the problem is solved, and the function stops calling itself. An algorithm that follows these rules satisfies the three laws of recursion:

1. A recursive algorithm must have a base case.
2. A recursive algorithm must change its state and move toward the base case.
3. A recursive algorithm must call itself, recursively.[14]

Here is a recursive algorithm that prints the lyrics to the popular folk song "99 Bottles of Beer on the Wall":

```
1   # http://tinyurl.com/z49qe4s
2
3
4   def bottles_of_beer(bob):
5       """ Prints 99 Bottle
6           of Beer on the
7           Wall lyrics.
8           :param bob: Must
9           be a positive
10          integer.
11      """
12      if bob < 1:
13          print("""No more
14                  bottles
15                  of beer
16                  on the wall.
17                  No more
18                  bottles of
19                  beer.""")
20          return
21      tmp = bob
22      bob -= 1
23      print("""{} bottles of
24              beer on the
25              wall. {} bottles
26              of beer. Take one
27              down, pass it
28              around, {} bottles
29              of beer on the
30              wall.
31          """.format(tmp,
32                      tmp,
33                      bob))
34      bottles_of_beer(bob)
35
36
37
38
39  bottles_of_beer(99)
```

```
>> 99 bottles of beer on the wall. 99 bottles of beer.
Take one down, pass it around, 98 bottles of beer on the
wall. 98 bottles of beer on the wall. 98 bottles of beer.
Take one down, pass it around, 97 bottles of beer on the wall.
...
No more bottles of beer on the wall. No more bottles of beer.
```

In this example, the first law of recursion was satisfied with the following base case:

```
1  # http://tinyurl.com/h4k3ytt
2
3
4  if bob < 1:
5      print("""No more
6          bottles
7          of beer
8          on the wall.
9          No more
10         bottles of
11         beer.""")
12     return
```

When the variable bob becomes less than 1, the function returns and stops calling itself.

The line bob -= 1 satisfies the second law of recursion because decrementing the variable bob moves toward your base case. In this example, you passed the number 99 to your function as a parameter. The base case is satisfied when the variable bob is less than 1, and every time the function calls itself, it moves toward its base case.

The final law of recursion is satisfied with:

```
1  # http://tinyurl.com/j7zwm8t
2
3
4  bottles_of_beer(bob)
```

This line ensures that as long as the base case is not satisfied, your function will call itself. Each time the function calls itself, it passes itself a parameter that has been decremented by 1, and thus moves toward the base case. The first time the function calls itself with this line, it will pass itself 98 as a parameter, then 97, then 96, until finally, it passes itself a parameter less than 1, which satisfies the base case and No more bottles of beer on the wall.

`No more bottles of beer.` prints. The function then hits the `return` keyword, which stops the algorithm.

Recursion is notoriously one of the toughest concepts for new programmers to grasp. If it is confusing to you at first, don't worry—keep practicing. And remember: to understand recursion; first you must understand recursion.

Vocabulary

Algorithm: A series of steps that can be followed to solve a problem.
Search algorithm: An algorithm that finds information in a data structure (like a list).
Sequential search: A simple search algorithm for finding information in a data structure that checks each item in it to see if it matches what it is looking for.
Palindrome: A word spelled the same forward and backward.
Anagram: A word created by rearranging the letters of another word.
Recursion: A method of solving problems by breaking the problem up into smaller and smaller pieces until it can be easily solved.
Iterative algorithm: Iterative algorithms solve problems by repeating steps over and over, typically using a loop.
Recursive algorithm: Recursive algorithms solve problems using functions that call themselves.
Base case: A condition that ends a recursive algorithm.

Challenge

1. Sign up for an account at http://leetcode.com, and try to solve three of their easy-level algorithm problems.

Part V
Landing a Job

Chapter 23. Best Programming Practices

"Always code as if the guy who ends up maintaining your code will be a violent psychopath who knows where you live."
—John Woods

Production code is the code in a product people use. When you put software into **production**, it means putting it out in the world. In this chapter, I cover a few general programming principles that will help you write production-ready code. Many of these principles originated in *The Pragmatic Programmer* by Andy Hunt and Dave Thomas, a book that dramatically improved the quality of my code.

Write Code as a Last Resort

Your job as a software engineer is to write as little code as possible. When you have a problem, your first thought should not be "How can I solve this?" It should be, "Has someone else solved this problem already, and can I use their solution?" If you are trying to solve a common problem, chances are someone else has already figured it out. Start by looking online for a solution. Only after you've determined no one else has already solved the problem should you start solving it yourself.

DRY

DRY is a programming principle that stands for Don't Repeat Yourself. Do not repeat the same, or nearly the same, code in a program. Instead, put the code into one function that can handle multiple situations.

Orthogonality

Orthogonality is another important programming principle popularized by The Pragmatic Programmer. Hunt and Thomas explain, "In computing, the term has come to signify a kind of independence or decoupling. Two or more things are orthogonal if changes in one do not affect any of the others. In a well-designed system, the database code will be orthogonal to the user interface: you can change the interface without affecting the database, and swap databases without changing the interface."[15] Put this in practice by remembering as much as possible that "a should not affect b." If you have two modules —module a and module b—module a should not make changes to things in module b, and vice versa. If you design a system where a affects b; which affects c; which affects d; things quickly spiral out of control and the system becomes unmanageable.

Every Piece of Data Should Have One Representation

When you have a piece of data, you should only store it in one location. For example, say you are building software that works with phone numbers. If you have two functions that both need to use a list of area codes, make sure there is only one list of area codes in your program. You should not have two duplicated lists of area codes, one for each function. Instead, you should have a global variable that holds the area codes. Or better yet, store the information in a file or a database.

The problem with duplicating data is at some point you will need to change it, and you will have to remember to alter the data in every place you duplicated it. If you change your area codes list in one function and forget the other function also uses the data, your program will not work properly. You can avoid this by only having one representation for every piece of data.

Functions Should Do One Thing

Every function you write should do one thing, and one thing only. If you find your functions getting too long, ask yourself if it is accomplishing more than one task. Limiting functions to accomplishing one task offers several advantages. Your code will be easier to read because the name of your function will describe exactly what it does. If your code isn't working it will be easier to debug because every function is responsible for a specific task, so you can quickly isolate and diagnose the function that isn't working. Best summarized by many famous programmers, "So much complexity in software comes from trying to make one thing do two things."

If It's Taking Too Long, You Are Probably Making a Mistake

If you are not working on something obviously complex, like working with large amounts of data, and your program is taking a very long time to load, assume you are doing something wrong.

Do Things the Best Way the First Time

If you are programming and you think, "I know there is a better way of doing this, but I'm in the middle of coding and don't want to stop and figure out how to do it better." Don't keep coding. Stop. Do it better.

Follow Conventions

Taking time to learn the conventions of the new programming language will help you read code written in the new language faster. PEP 8 is a set of guidelines for writing Python code, and you should read it. It includes the rules for extending Python code to new lines. It's available at https://www.python.org/dev/peps/pep-0008/.

Use a Powerful IDE

Thus far, you've been using IDLE, the IDE that comes with Python, to write your code. But IDLE is just one of many IDEs available, and I do not recommend using it long term because it is not very powerful. For example, if you open up a Python project in a better IDE, there will be different tabs for each Python file. In IDLE you have to open a new window for each file, which is tedious and makes it difficult to navigate back and forth between files.

I use an IDE called PyCharm created by JetBrains. They offer a free version as well as a professional version. I made a list of the features of PyCharm that save me the most time:

1. If you would like to see the definition of a variable, function, or object, PyCharm has a shortcut that jumps to the the code that defined it (even if it is in a different file). There is also a shortcut to jump back to the page you started from.

2. PyCharm has a feature that saves local history, which has dramatically improved my productivity. PyCharm automatically saves a new version of your project every time it changes. You can use PyCharm as local version control system without having to push to a repository. You don't have to do anything; it happens automatically. Before I knew about this feature, I would often solve a problem, change the solution, and then decide I wanted to go back to the original solution. If I didn't push the initial solution to GitHub, it was long gone, and I would have to rewrite it again. With this feature, you can jump back in time 10 minutes and reload your project exactly how it was. If you change your mind again, you can jump back and forth between different solutions as many times as you want.

3. In your workflow, you are probably copying and pasting code a lot. In PyCharm, instead of copying and pasting, you can move code up and down on the page you are on.

4. PyCharm supports version control systems like Git and SVN. Instead of going to the command-line, you can use Git from PyCharm. The fewer trips you have to make back and forth between your IDE and the command-line, the more productive you will be.

5. PyCharm has a built-in command-line and Python Shell.

6. PyCharm has a built-in **debugger**. A debugger is a program that allows you to stop the execution of your code and move through your program line by line so you can see the values of the variables in your code at different parts of your program.

If you are interested in learning to use PyCharm, JetBrains has a tutorial available at https://www.jetbrains.com/help/pycharm/2016.1/quick-start-guide.html.

Logging

Logging is the practice of recording data when your software runs. You can use logging to help debug your program and gain additional insight into what happened when your program ran. Python comes with a logging `module` that lets you log to the console or a file.

When something goes wrong in your program, you don't want it to go unnoticed—you should log information about what happened to review later. Logging is also useful for collecting and analyzing data. For example, you might set up a web server to log data— including the date and time—every time it receives a request. You could store all of your logs in a database, and create another program to analyze the data and create a graph displaying the times of day people visit your website.

The blogger Henrik Warne writes, "One of the differences between a great programmer and a bad programmer is that a great programmer adds logging and tools that make it easy to debug the program when things fail." You can learn how to use Python's `logging` module at https://docs.python.org/3/howto/logging.html.

Testing

Testing a program means checking that the program "meets the requirements that guided its design and development, responds correctly to all kinds of inputs, performs its functions within an acceptable time, is sufficiently usable, can be installed and run in its intended environments, and achieves the general result its stakeholders desire."[16] To test their programs, programmers write more programs.

In a production environment, testing is not optional. You should consider every program you intend to put into production incomplete until you have written tests for it. However, if you write a quick program you are never going to use again, testing might be a waste of time. If you are writing a program that other people are going to use, you should write tests. As several famous programmers have said, "Untested code is broken code." You can learn how to use Python's `unittest` module at https://docs.python.org/3/library/unittest.html.

Code Reviews

In a **code review** someone reads your code and gives feedback. You should do as many code reviews as you can—especially as a self-taught programmer. Even if you follow all the best practices laid out in this chapter, you are going to do things incorrectly. You need someone with experience to read over your code and tell you the mistakes you are making, so you can fix them.

Code Review is a website where you can get code reviews from a community of programmers. Anyone can go on Code Review and post their code. Other members of the Stack Exchange community review your code, give you feedback about what you did well, and offer helpful suggestions on how you can improve. You can visit Code Review at http://codereview.stackexchange.com/.

Security

Security is an easy subject for the self-taught programmer to ignore. You probably won't be asked about security in interviews, and security is not important for the programs you write while you are learning to program. However, once you get your first programming job, you are directly responsible for the security of the code you write. In this section, I provide some tips to keep your code safe.

Earlier, you learned to use `sudo` to issue a command as the root user. Never run a program from the command-line using `sudo` if you don't have to because a hacker will have root access if they compromise the program. You should also disable root logins if you are managing a server. Every hacker is aware there is a root account, so it is an easy target when attacking a system.

Always assume user input is malicious. Several kinds of malicious attacks rely on exploiting programs that accept user input, so you should also assume all user input is malicious and program accordingly.

Another strategy for keeping your software secure is to minimize your **attack surface**—the different areas of your program where attackers could extract data or attack your system. By making your attack area as small as possible, you reduce the likelihood of vulnerabilities in your program. Some strategies for minimizing your attack surface: avoid storing confidential data if you don't have to, give users the lowest level of access you can, use as few third-party libraries as possible (the less code, the less amount of possible exploits), and get rid of features that are no longer being used (less code, less exploits).

Avoiding logging in as the root user on your system, not trusting user input, and minimizing your attack surface are important steps to making sure your programs are secure. But these are just starting points. You should always try to think like a hacker. How would a hacker exploit your code? Thinking like this can help you find vulnerabilities you otherwise would overlook. There is a lot more to learn about security than I can cover in this book, so always be thinking and learning about it. Bruce Schneier said it best "Security is a state of mind."

Vocabulary

Production code: The code in a product people use.

Production: When you put software into production, it means putting it out in the world.

DRY: A programming principle that stands for Don't Repeat Yourself.

Orthogonality: "In computing, the term has come to signify a kind of independence or decoupling. Two or more things are orthogonal if changes in one do not affect any of the others. In a well-designed system, the database code will be orthogonal to the user interface: you can change the interface without affecting the database, and swap databases without changing the interface."[17]

Debugger: A debugger is a program that allows you to stop the execution of your code and move through your program line by line so you can see the values of the variables in your code at different parts of your program.

Logging: The practice of recording data when your software runs.

Testing: Checking that the program "meets the requirements that guided its design and development, responds correctly to all kinds of inputs, performs its functions within an acceptable time, is sufficiently usable, can be installed and run in its intended environments, and achieves the general result its stakeholders desire."[18]

Code review: When someone reads your code and gives you feedback.

Attack surface: The different areas of your program where attackers could extract data or attack your system.

Chapter 24. Your First Programming Job

"Beware of 'the real world.' A speaker's appeal to it is always an invitation not to challenge his tacit assumptions."
— Edsger W. Dijkstra

The final part of this book is dedicated to helping you with your career. Getting your first programming job requires extra effort, but if you follow my advice, you should have no problem. Luckily, once you land your first programming job and get some experience, when it comes time to look for your next job, recruiters will be reaching out to you.

Choose a Path

When you apply for a programming job, you will be expected to know a particular set of technologies, depending on the domain the job is in. While it's fine to be a generalist (a programmer who dabbles in everything) while you are learning to program, and it is possible to get a job as a generalist programmer, you should probably focus on an area of programming you enjoy and become an expert in it. Focusing on one programming path will make getting a job easier.

Web and mobile development are two of the most popular programming paths. There are two specialties within them: front end and the back end. The front end of an application is the part you can see—like the GUI of a web app. The back end is what you can't see—the part that provides the front end with data. The titles for open programming jobs will read something like "Python Backend Programmer," which means they are looking for someone who programs the backend of a website and is familiar with Python. The job description will list the technologies the ideal candidate will be familiar with, along with any additional skills needed.

Some companies have a team devoted to the front end and another to the back end. Other companies only hire full stack developers—programmers that can work on both the front and back ends; however, this only applies to companies building websites or apps.

There are many other programming areas you can work in, such as security, platform engineering, and data science. Job descriptions on sites listing programming jobs are a good place to learn more about the requirements of different areas of programming. The Python Job Board, found at https://www.python.org/jobs, is a good place to start. Read the requirements for a few jobs, as well as the technologies they use, to get an idea what you need to learn to be competitive for the type of job you want.

Getting Initial Experience

Before you are hired for your first programming job, you will need experience. But how do you get programming experience if no one will hire you without it? There are a few ways to solve this problem. You can get involved in open source by starting an open source project or contributing to the thousands of open source projects on GitHub.

Another option is to do freelance work. Create a profile on a site similar to Upwork, and start applying for small programming jobs. I recommend finding someone you know who needs some programming work done, have them sign up for an Upwork account, then officially hire you there so they can leave you a great review for your work. Until you have at least one good review on a site like Upwork, it is hard to get hired for jobs. Once people see that you've successfully completed at least one job, getting hired becomes easier, because you've established some credibility.

Getting an Interview

Once you've gained programming experience through either open source or freelance work, it's time to start interviewing. I've found the most efficient way to get an interview is to focus on LinkedIn. If you don't have a LinkedIn account, create one to start networking with potential employers. Write a summary about yourself at the top of your profile, and make sure to highlight your programming skills. For example, a lot of people say something like "Programming Languages: Python, JavaScript" at the top of their profile, which helps lead recruiters searching for those keywords to them. Make sure to put your open source or freelancing experience as your most recent job.

Once your profile is complete, start connecting with technical recruiters—there are lots of technical recruiters on LinkedIn. They are always looking for new talent and will be eager to connect with you. Once they accept your invitation, reach out and ask if they are hiring for any open positions.

The Interview

If a recruiter thinks you are a good fit for the role they are hiring for, they will send you a message on LinkedIn asking to set up a phone screen. The phone screen will be with the recruiter, so it is usually non-technical, although I've had recruiters ask me technical questions they've memorized the answer to during first interviews. The conversation is about the technologies you know, your previous experience, and figuring out if you would fit in with the company's culture.

If you do well, you will advance to the second round—a technical phone screen—where you speak with members of the engineering team. They will ask you the same questions from the first interview. However, this time the questions are accompanied by a technical test over the phone. The engineers will give you the address of a website where they have posted programming questions, and ask you to solve them.

If you make it past the second round, you will usually have a third interview. The third interview is typically in person at the company's office. Like the first two, you meet with different engineers on the team. They ask about your skills and experience and administer more technical tests. Sometimes you stay for lunch to see how you interact with the team. The third round is where the famous whiteboard coding tests happen. If the company you are interviewing for does whiteboarding, you will be asked to solve several programming problems. I recommend buying a whiteboard and practicing beforehand because solving a programming problem on a whiteboard is much harder than solving it on a computer.

Hacking the Interview

The majority of programming interviews focus on two subjects—data structures and algorithms. To pass your programming interview, you know exactly what you must do— get very good at these two specific areas of computer science. Fortunately, this will help you to become a better programmer.

You can narrow down the questions to focus on even further by thinking about the interview from the interviewer's perspective. Think about the situation your interviewer is in; they say software is never complete, and it's true. Your interviewer most likely has a lot of work and doesn't want to dedicate a lot of time interviewing candidates. Are they going to spend their valuable time coming up with original programming questions? Probably not. They are going to Google "programming interview questions," and ask one of the first ones they find. This situation leads to the same interview questions coming up over and over again—and there are some great resources out there to practice them! I highly recommend using LeetCode—I've found every question anyone has ever asked me in a programming interview there.

Chapter 25. Working on a Team

"You can't have great software without a great team, and most software teams behave like dysfunctional families."
— Jim McCarthy

Coming from a self-taught background, you will be used to programming alone. Once you join a company, you need to learn how to work on a team. Even if you start a company, eventually you will hire additional programmers, at which point you will need to learn to work as a team. Programming is a team sport, and like any team sport, you need to get along with your teammates. This chapter provides some tips for successfully working in a team environment.

Master the Basics

When a company hires you, you are expected to be competent in the skills covered in this book. It is not enough to simply read this book—you need to master the concepts as well. Your teammates will get frustrated if they are constantly helping you with the basics.

Don't Ask What You Can Google

As a new, self-taught member of a programming team, you will have plenty to learn and need to ask a lot of questions. Asking questions is a great way to learn, but you want to make sure you are asking the right questions. Only ask a question if you've spent at least five minutes Googling the answer yourself. If you ask too many questions you could have easily figured out on your own, you will annoy your teammates.

Changing Code

By reading this book, you've demonstrated you are the type of person who is constantly looking to improve. Unfortunately, not everyone on your team will share your enthusiasm for becoming a better programmer. Many programmers don't have the desire to keep learning—they are fine doing things suboptimally.

Bad code is especially prevalent in startups, where shipping code quickly is often more important than shipping high-quality code. If you find yourself in this situation, tread lightly. Changing someone's code may hurt their ego. Even worse, if you spend a lot of time fixing other people's code, you will not have enough time to contribute to new projects, and it may look like you are not working hard enough. The best way to avoid this environment is to carefully question any company you are interviewing with about their engineering culture.

If you still find yourself in this situation, it is best to listen to Edward Yourdon, "If you think your management doesn't know what it's doing or that your organization turns out low-quality software crap that embarrasses you, then leave."

Imposter Syndrome

Everyone who programs feels overwhelmed sometimes, and no matter how hard you work there are going to be things you don't know. As a self-taught programmer, it is especially easy to feel inadequate because someone asked you to do something you've never heard of, or you feel like there are many concepts in computer science you still do not understand. These things happen to everyone—not just you.

I was surprised when my friend with a master's degree in computer science from Stanford told me he felt this way as well. He said everyone in his program dealt with imposter syndrome. He noticed they reacted one of two ways: they either stayed humble and were willing to admit when they didn't know something—and worked to learn it, or they pretended they knew everything (when they didn't) and stifled their learning. Remember you got to where you are by working hard, and it's OK if you don't know everything, nobody does. Just stay humble, and relentlessly study anything you don't understand, and you will be unstoppable.

Chapter 26. Further Learning

"The best programmers are not marginally better than merely good ones. They are an order-of-magnitude better, measured by whatever standard: conceptual creativity, speed, ingenuity of design, or problem-solving ability."
— Randall E. Stross

The article "ABC: Always Be Coding" by David Byttow gives great advice on how to get a job as a software engineer. The title says it all—always be coding. You can find the article at https://medium.com/always-be-coding/abc-always-be-coding-d5f8051afce2#.2hjho0px7. If you combine ABC with a new acronym I made up—ABL—always be learning—you are sure to have an exceptional career. In this chapter, I am going to review some of the programming resources I've found helpful.

The Classics

There are a few programming books that are considered must-reads. *The Pragmatic Programmer* by Andy Hunt and Dave Thomas; *Design Patterns* by Erich Gamma, John Vlissides, Ralph Johnson, and Richard Helm (design patterns are an important subject I didn't get a chance to cover) ; *Code Complete* by Steve McConnell; *Compilers: Principles, Techniques, and Tools* by Alfred Aho, Jeffrey Ullman, Monica S. Lam, and Ravi Sethi; and *Introduction to Algorithms* by the MIT Press. I also highly recommend *Problem Solving with Data Structures and Algorithms*, a free, interactive, excellent introduction to algorithms by Bradley N. Miller and David L. Ranum and much easier to understand than MIT's *Introduction to Algorithms*.

Online Classes

Online coding classes are another way to improve your programming skills. You can find all of my class recommendations at http://theselftaughtprogrammer.io/courses.

Hacker News

Hacker News is a platform for user-submitted news hosted on the technology incubator Y Combinator's website, found at https://news.ycombinator.com. It will help you keep up to date with the newest trends and technologies.

Chapter 27. Next Steps

"Love the little trade which thou hast learned, and be content therewith."
—Marcus Aurelius

First of all—thank you for purchasing this book. I hope it's helped you become a better programmer. Now that you're finished, it's time for you to get down to business. Where do you go from here? Data structures and algorithms. Get on LeetCode and practice those algorithms. Then practice them some more! In this chapter, I give some final thoughts on how you can continue to improve as a programmer (once you finished practicing writing algorithms.

Find a Mentor

A mentor will help take your programming skills to the next level. One of the hard things about learning to program is that there are so many things you can do suboptimally without knowing it. I mentioned earlier you can help combat this by doing code reviews. A mentor can do code reviews with you to help improve your coding process, recommend books, and teach you programming concepts you don't understand.

Strive to Go Deep

There is a concept in programming called a "black box," which refers to something you use but do not understand how it works. When you first start programming, everything is a black box. One of the best ways to get better at programming is to open up every black box you find and try to understand how it works. One of my friends told me it was a major "aha" moment when he realized the command-line itself is a program. Opening up a black box is what I call going deep.

Writing this book helped me go deep. There were certain concepts I thought I understood, only to find out I couldn't explain them. I had to go deep. Don't stop at just one answer, read all the explanations on a topic you can find. Ask questions and read differing opinions online.

Another way to go deep is to build things you want to understand better. Having trouble understanding version control? Build a simple version control system in your free time. Taking the time to do a project like that is well worth the investment—it will improve your understanding of whatever you are struggling with.

Other Advice

I once came across a forum topic discussing different ways to become a better programmer. The top voted answer was surprising: Do things other than programming. I've found this to be true—reading books like The Talent Code by Daniel Coyle has made me a better programmer because he lays out exactly what you need to do to master any skill. Keep your eye out for things outside of programming you can bring to your programming game.

The last piece of advice I will leave you with is to spend as much time as you can reading other people's code. It is one of the best ways to improve as a programmer. When you are learning, make sure to strike a balance between writing and reading code. Reading other people's code is going to be difficult at first, but it is important because you can learn so much from other programmers.

I hope you enjoyed reading this book as much as I enjoyed writing it. Please feel free to email me at cory@theselftaughtprogrammer.io for any reason. I also have a programming newsletter you can sign up for at http://theselftaughtprogrammer.io and a Facebook group located at https://www.facebook.com/groups/selftaughtprogrammers where you can get in touch with me and a community of other people learning to program. If you like this book, please consider leaving a review on Amazon at https://www.amazon.com/dp/B01M01YDQA#customerReviews, it helps get this book in the hands of more people, and I appreciate every review I receive. Best of luck on the rest of your journey.

Acknowledgements

I want to thank everyone that helped make this book possible. My parents, Abby and James Althoff, were so supportive during the entire process. My Dad went through every page of the book and gave me amazing feedback. I couldn't have made this happen without him. My girlfriend, Lauren Wordell, put up with me working on this book at all times. I want to thank my incredibly talented illustrator Blake Bowers; my editors Steve Bush, Madeline Luce, Pam Walatka and Lawrence Sanfilippo; and my friend Antoine Sindu—several of our discussions made it into the book. I also want to thank Randee Fenner, who supported the project on Kickstarter and introduced me to Pam. Shoutout to my former boss Anzar Afaq, who was incredibly supportive when I joined his team at eBay. A big thank you to all of the beta readers who read the book early and gave me feedback. Finally, I want to thank everyone on Kickstarter that backed this project, especially Jin Chun, Sunny Lee, and Leigh Forrest. Thank you all so much!

Citations

1. https://www.infoworld.com/article/2908474/application-development/stack-overflow-survey-finds-nearly-half-have-no-degree-in-computer-science.html

2. http://www.wsj.com/articles/computer-programming-is-a-trade-lets-act-like-it-1407109947?mod=e2fb

3. https://en.wikipedia.org/wiki/Syntax

4. https://en.wikipedia.org/wiki/Syntax

5. https://www.tutorialspoint.com/python/python_files_io.htm

6. https://maryrosecook.com/blog/post/a-practical-introduction-to-functionalprogramming

7. http://whatis.techtarget.com/definition/abstraction

8. http://stackoverflow.com/questions/1031273/what-is-polymorphism-what-is-it-forand-how-is-it-used

9. http://stackoverflow.com/questions/1031273/what-is-polymorphism-what-is-it-forand-how-is-it-used

10. http://whatis.techtarget.com/definition/abstraction

11. https://en.wikipedia.org/wiki/Regular_expression

12. http://tldp.org/LDP/Bash-Beginners-Guide/html/sect_04_01.html

13. https://en.wikipedia.org/wiki/Regular_expression

14. http://interactivepython.org/runestone/static/pythonds/Recursion/TheThreeLawsof-Recursion.html

15. The Pragmatic Programmer

16. https://en.wikipedia.org/wiki/Software_testing

17. https://students.cs.byu.edu/~cs340ta/fall2017/notes/06-DesignPrinciples/OLD/More-DesignPrinciples.pdf

18. https://en.wikipedia.org/wiki/Software_testing

Index

A

B

C

characteristics, 14, 154, 162
characters, 247
classname, 144
clause, 41-42, 44, 62
clauses, 41-42
clients, 153
code, 35, 108, 124
codebase, 213, 223
codereview, 257
commandline, 183-184
compilers, 265
complexity, 141, 254
computer, 1-3, 5-8, 10-11, 18, 119,
    123, 128-129, 132, 145, 183-187,
    190, 192, 209-210, 213, 215,
    217, 224, 232, 261, 264
computers, 5, 8, 213
concatenation, 89, 101
conditional, 35, 44
conditionally, 35, 44
constants, 20
container, 67, 70, 73, 76, 85, 126
containers, 67, 80, 85
convention, 47, 49, 65, 143
conventions, 153, 255
cory, 221, 268
coryalthoff, 25, 186, 189, 191,
    219-221, 223
courier, 14
coyle, 137, 268
css, 225
csv, 126-129
cunningham, 171

D

data, 2, 7, 18-21, 23, 43, 52, 54,
    64-65, 67, 69, 75-76, 85, 106,
    123, 126, 128-129, 139, 141-143,
    151-155, 162, 164-165, 183, 186,
    190, 193, 195, 209, 212-213,
    216, 224-230, 233, 237, 242,
    244, 251, 254-259, 261, 265, 267
database, 7, 253-254, 256, 258
databases, 253, 258
debug, 254, 256
debugger, 256, 258
dec, 9, 221
decimal, 19, 43
declarations, 21
decoupling, 253, 258
decrement, 22-23, 44
decremented, 109, 250
decrementing, 22, 250
decrements, 109
def, 48-51, 54, 56-60, 64, 120, 132,
    135, 140, 142-148, 151-153,
    157-161, 164-168, 171-172,
    174-176, 178-180, 204, 211,
    227-229, 234, 236, 238, 240,
    243, 245-247, 249
del, 79
delimiter, 126-128
delta, 215, 219-220, 223
dependencies, 209, 212
dequeue, 237-241
developers, 5, 64, 209, 259
dict, 76-79, 247

dictionaries, 67, 75-77, 85, 213, 224, 233

dictionary, 76-80, 82, 84-85, 104, 114, 247

diff, 222-223

directories, 185-187, 189, 193

directory, 124, 185-193, 195-196, 210, 213, 215-217, 224

division, 26-29, 61

docs, 117, 211-212, 256

docstring, 64, 66

docstrings, 64-66

documentation, 184

dorsey, 3

E

ebay, 1, 3, 269

elif, 35, 38-40, 42, 44, 140, 243

ellipses, 14

elsestatement, 35-36, 38, 44, 54-55

empty, 233-238, 240-242

encapsulate, 54

encapsulation, 151, 153, 162

enqueue, 237-240

epoch, 241-242

equality, 32

equations, 29

error, 9, 25-26, 44, 61-62, 66, 87, 96-97, 117

errors, 25-26, 60, 141-142

evaluation, 34, 110

excel, 126-128

exception, 25-26, 44, 53, 56, 58-59, 62, 64, 66, 70-71, 74, 79, 88, 95, 117

exceptions, 25-26, 62-63, 66

execute, 7, 11, 17, 35-37, 42, 44, 47, 62, 65, 67, 103, 108, 185

executed, 35-36, 38-39, 62, 103, 111, 196

executes, 37-38, 62, 103, 108-109, 111, 114, 120, 125, 144, 183, 192, 196

executing, 242

execution, 256, 258

exponentiation, 28

exponents, 29

expression, 29-31, 34-38, 44, 108-110, 114, 167-168, 172, 195-197, 199-203, 205-206

expressions, 2, 29, 32-34, 37-39, 44, 183, 195, 197, 199, 202, 205-206

F

faulkner, 91-92

fenner, 269

ferriss, 4

fifo, 237, 242

file, 125, 217

filepath, 125, 196

filepaths, 123

G

H

I

mkdir, 187-188
module, 10, 117-121, 123, 126-127,
    149, 174, 197, 206, 209-211,
    226-227, 241-242, 253, 256
modules, 117-119, 121, 212, 253
modulo, 27, 61, 111, 243
multiline, 199-200
multiplication, 29, 90, 101
mutable, 70, 76-77, 85, 105-106

N

name, 10-11, 21, 24, 43, 48-49, 56,
    59-60, 64, 70, 77, 80, 103-104,
    117, 121, 125, 143-145, 161,
    163-164, 166, 168, 175-177, 179,
    186-187, 189-192, 210-212
nameerror, 59-60, 64
namespaces, 196, 199-200
new, 145
newline, 98, 127
nonetype, 20, 43
nongreedy, 203
noun, 92, 204-205
number, 204, 245

O

object, 145
objectoriented, 139, 151, 154, 162
odd, 28, 37, 40, 42, 54-56
operand, 44, 167
operands, 29, 31, 44, 167
operations, 22, 29, 44, 73, 191, 193
operator, 21, 27-32, 43-44, 71,
    89-90, 167, 223, 243
operators, 26, 28-29, 32, 44, 168,
    172
oranges, 142-143, 146-147
oriented, 2, 139, 141-142, 148-149,
    151, 160, 162-163
orthogonal, 253, 258
orthogonality, 253, 258
override, 159, 166
overrides, 160
overriding, 159, 162
overrode, 166

P

package, 183, 209-212
palindrome, 245-246, 251
paradigm, 139, 142, 149
paradigms, 2, 139, 141
param, 64, 204, 249

Q

R

T

tag, 226, 228-230

tinyurl, 7, 11, 13-43, 45, 48-85,
    87-101, 103-113, 115, 117-121,
    123-129, 132-136, 139-140,
    142-149, 151-169, 171, 173-175,
    177, 184-191, 193, 196-207,
    209-212, 215-223, 225-230,
    234-236, 238-240, 242-243,
    245-247, 249-250

torvalds, 1, 195, 233

tuple, 73-75, 77-78, 82, 84-85, 104,
    114, 153, 165

tuples, 67, 69, 73, 76, 85, 87, 89,
    153, 233

tutorialspoint, 62

twitter, 3

typeerror, 74

U

ubuntu, 5, 8, 183-184, 196, 210,
    212, 226

underscore, 24, 131-132, 134, 143,
    153-154, 203

underscores, 49, 134, 143-144,
    203-205

unix, 5, 6, 8, 123, 183, 186-187,
    189-193, 195-196, 210, 226

upwork, 260

url, 14, 215-216, 228-229

urllib, 227-229

urlopen, 227-229

urls, 216, 226-228

V

valueerror, 53, 63, 95

variable, 24, 103, 125, 143-145,
    163, 190

variables, 20, 22-24, 32, 35, 44-45,
    57-60, 64, 67, 117, 139-141,
    144-146, 148-149, 151, 153, 156,
    158, 162-164, 168-169, 172-173,
    175, 177, 190, 193, 196, 228,
    256, 258

virtualenvs, 212

W

waitzkin, 3

walatka, 269

web, 8, 14, 183-184, 191, 209, 211,
    225-226, 229-230, 256, 259

website, 5-6, 137, 209, 211-215,
    219, 224-228, 230, 256-257, 259,
    261, 265

websites, 210, 225-226, 259

whileloop, 108-111, 113, 242

Y

Z

Printed in the USA
CPSIA information can be obtained
at www.ICGtesting.com
LVHW051119240923
759163LV00007B/542